I Learned to Dance in Reform School

By

H.L. McCall

Text copyright 2018 H.L. McCall

All Rights Reserved

This book is dedicated to Ruby Alberta Miller, a wonderful, beloved friend and mentor, who spent her life trying to reach and save lost young people. Rest in peace, Ruby – I love you!

Table of Contents

CHAPTER 1 9

CHAPTER 2 16

CHAPTER 3 23

CHAPTER 4 37

CHAPTER 5 44

CHAPTER 6 48

CHAPTER 7 59

CHAPTER 8 70

CHAPTER 9 80

CHAPTER 10 88

CHAPTER 11 99

CHAPTER 12 106

CHAPTER 13 115

CHAPTER 14 124

CHAPTER 15 137

CHAPTER 16	144
CHAPTER 17	148
CHAPTER 18	159
CHAPTER 19	163
CHAPTER 20	178
CHAPTER 21	184
CHAPTER 22	191
CHAPTER 23	203
CHAPTER 24	210
CHAPTER 25	216
CHAPTER 26	226
CHAPTER 27	236
CHAPTER 28	248
CHAPTER 29	258
CHAPTER 30	270
CHAPTER 31	283

CHAPTER 32 .... **310**

Chapter 1

    I was a rumor in my family. None of them knew for certain, but the rumor was that "crazy" Helen had a daughter. No one knew who, or where, I was, nor did they care to find out about me. I really didn't know them either, except for stories my mother told me about my grandfather and his family. So having a family wasn't a reality for me. I didn't know what family was, so I didn't miss it. The reality was just me and my mother. I did have my grandfather's picture to moon over and feel like he belonged to me somehow.

Mom said she had an aunt who died in a mental institution in Montana when she, (mom) was a young girl. Aside from the aunt, her family from both parents included a long line of well educated, busy people who were involved in their own lives, and were not too interested in "crazy Helen" or her lonely little daughter.

No telling how much, of how my mother was, was genetic and how much was brain damage from a car accident that happened when she was a two-month-old baby. Her parents had her lying in the back seat of an open car. That's what they called a car with no doors back then. When her father turned a corner a little too fast, she slid out onto the road, causing brain damage and grand mal epileptic seizures. Can't remember who told me about that.

I was told about my existence being a rumor in the family by a woman who was the granddaughter of my grandfather's brother. I had taken a notion a few years ago to try and find some of my relatives, wanting to learn more about my background. When I found this woman, that's what she told me. It stunned me a little, and hurt my feelings, I have to admit.

Because I was excited about meeting one of my relatives, I assumed they would be interested in meeting me, too. Not the case. She couldn't wait to get shed of me. I guess she didn't want to be saddled with one of the crazy relatives in the family. Also, to give her a break, she was having serious health problems, and was bedridden. She probably didn't need some unknown relative popping into her life at that point.

I'll never forget my first view of the Vocational School for Girls, the state of Montana's reform school for girls. I got it from the back seat of a 1954 Chevy sedan, as Bill Jones, the truant officer from Havre, Montana, and his wife, drove me onto the campus.

I was 13 years old, and didn't much care what was done with me. I looked around with mild interest, as we drove down the lane leading to the main building. This was to be the first real home I'd ever had. I had no idea what I was getting into.

The "cottages", where the girls lived, were huge two-story brick buildings, with gables looming high on top of them. They were scattered along a curving driveway that ran the length of the ten-acre property. There were four buildings in all.

Beautifully groomed hedges lined the drive. Big elm trees decorated a small park, with a creek running through it. The girls called this "the swamp" and told all newcomers that if they went in there and they got stuck in the creek, they'd sink into quicksand and there was no way to get them out.

Not true, but who was going to be brave enough to disprove the myth? I never was, even as an adult. Mental pictures like that stick no matter how much logic gets involved. Sinking into quicksand is a very scary idea.

The administration building was a tall, two-story brick structure, and its many windows stared coldly at us as the little car pulled up in front of it. Big wide cement stairs led to a porch that ran halfway across the front of the building.

The cottages and the administration building had the same wide staircase, and the same basic design. The gym had the big porch, and a simple set of stairs that led out the side of the building. They were very handy for little juvenile delinquent girls that wanted to run away on a beautiful spring day. But we'll talk more about that later.

Mr. Jones and his wife had been very kind and friendly to me, as we drove the nearly three hundred miles from Havre to Helena, the state capital. The truant officer and his wife were probably in their late 40's, which, of course, to me meant old. He was over-fed, and she was small, meek, and maybe just a little bit afraid of this 13-year-old tyrant.

They had told me the school was a nice place, the food was good, and the floors were clean enough to eat off of. I hadn't stooped to eating off floors at that point, but I suppose it could have come to that eventually, if they hadn't taken me out of my mother's reach and sent me to live at this school.

I was a wild kid at thirteen. I had had absolutely no guidance in my upbringing. My mother was barely into her teens mentally and emotionally, maybe not even that old. The only knowledge I really possessed was survival skills, and a love for music.

Mom was immature, spoiled by her father, and mentally ill. She grew worse as the years went by. I spent a lot of years angry at her, before I realized what her problem was.

I was in my middle forties when I finally figured it out, with help of a therapy group I was leading! I always thought she was just neglectful, childish, and didn't care about me. It sure flipped a switch in my reality when the lights went on.

My mother was born in 1912. She had come from a good, middle-class, family of newspaper people, teachers, and ministers. She didn't relate to anyone emotionally and never mentally grew to adulthood. She'd had polio when she was two years old, and that had crippled her whole left side. She walked with a heavy, dragging limp, and couldn't use her left hand. She was a survivor and tough, but she was also needy, wanting to be taken care of, and wasn't choosy about who it was doing the caretaking.

Her father, Haven, had been a newspaperman. He and my great-grandfather Mahood had partnered in starting and developing The Big Sandy, Montana Mountaineer newspaper. Later, Haven opened a printing shop in Great Falls. I don't know why he left Big Sandy.

Apparently, he thought he was going to live forever and be able to take care of his daughter. He had not allowed her to date in her teen years and didn't want to see her get married, so she had no guidance in how to choose a good husband, or deal with marriage and a kid. I think he wanted to prevent her from having children because he was afraid she'd have children like herself, and be a really bad mother. Also, I think there might have been a lot of guilt driving him. After all, he'd been the one driving the car that his baby girl fell out of.

Evidently a doctor back then wanted to operate on my mother's brain, and Haven refused to allow it. He wasn't willing to let medical people experiment with her. From everything I learned about him, he was a good father who sang to his wife and children in a beautiful professional voice. He and his brothers had sung as a trio in burlesque.

Back in the early 1900's, they had no way of knowing what was going on with people like my mother, and everybody just thought she was crazy.

Haven loved her and her brother. He just didn't know what to do with a child like her and he was highly protective. However, even with the problems she had, he made her stay in school until she finished high school. She was close to twenty when she graduated.

My grandfather died when my mother was 28 years old. She still lived at home and had never dated. Mom told me about a school teacher who wanted to court her. Haven threw him out and told him not to come back. I sure wish he would have allowed the romance to continue. I guess things happen the way they're supposed to, though.

Chapter 2

Within weeks after Haven's death from prostate cancer, mom met my father, and married him. He was a pin setter in one of the bowling alleys in Great Falls. His parents, she told me, were Irish immigrants. Turns out, they were German and from

Missouri. They had changed their name so as not to not be singled out. A year later I entered the world.

Not long after my birth, Louie, my father, was gone. My mother told me that he was a thief and liked to burglarize houses. On one of his raids, he brought her a fur coat he had stolen and she refused to keep it.

Then, one night he came home, got into a fight with her, and hit her over the head with a pitcher while she was feeding me. She got out of her chair, grabbed him by the arm with her right hand, and broke his arm. All the strength she would have had in her shriveled left arm gravitated to the right arm. He didn't stay around long after that. He left and she and I were on our own.

My mother had an older brother, Bob. Mom told me that he and his wife had wanted to adopt me when I was a baby and she wouldn't allow it. I think it was more out of pity for me. Later they had their own babies. When my mother refused to let them have me, they lost interest, and there was no one else to be there for my support except a step-grandmother. Marjorie was her name and she had her own problems with my mother and my grandfather's printing business.

Haven's brother insisted she pay him back money he loaned them to start the business, and he wanted it immediately. She had to sell the print shop to get the money.

Soon, my mom was married again to my father's brother Harry, making me my own cousin. Off they went to Missouri and wound up picking cotton. I was boarded out with some folks there. I was just a baby at the time. Harry, my uncle/stepfather, left mom and me there in Missouri and went his way. She then ran around with his other brother for a while and nearly married him. I can't remember that guy's name. If she had married him, I would have wound up being my own double cousin? Hmm. I was becoming my own family system.

Finally my mother gave up on the "McCall" brothers, and with me in tow, went back to Montana. She moved into a housing project called Parkdale in Great Falls, and went to work for the railroad shortly before the war ended. I was put into a nursery school.

My mother couldn't drive, so she got around on a bicycle. She would put me in the basket of her bike and take me downtown to stay in the nursery school while she went to work.

We'd have breakfast across the street from the Civic Center in a little corner restaurant. The nursery school was housed in the Civic Center, which also housed a movie theater, and I don't know what else. Mom would drop me off and go across the river to work.

I don't think my mother ever meant to be mean. She just didn't realize that other people had feelings, including little girls. Come to think of it, she didn't have much empathy for people in general.

For example, one morning in the restaurant, I had pancakes for breakfast. I picked up a jar of something and asked her what it was. She encouraged me to put some on my pancakes, so I did. She watched, and said nothing.

I took a bite, gagged and spit it out, coughing myself nearly sick. It was horse radish, and I'd gotten a big dose of it.

She and the other patrons in the place laughed and laughed over that. I didn't cry, but I still remember the shock, the hurt and humiliation, over the whole thing. They didn't even replace the pancakes, so I went without breakfast that morning. Funny the things you remember. I guess most of the adults didn't have much empathy for little kids back then. I wonder sometimes if they do even today.

My step-grandmother, Marjorie, hung around for a while and used to babysit me sometimes, when I was three and four years old. I remember one time she tried to wash my long hair by putting my head backward into the kitchen sink.

I couldn't stand getting water in my ears because of feeling horrible pain, and I screamed and cried and fought so much, she spanked me. I kept trying to tell her I wanted my head forward in the sink to keep the water out of my ears. She finally gave up and let me have my way. Nobody realized I had holes in my eardrums and was having hearing problems, a result of Rheumatic Fever when I was two or three.

My grandmother lived upstairs in an apartment in a big old mansion near downtown. One Saturday morning, I must have been maybe five or six years old, I heard on the news that a horse had escaped from the fairgrounds. The fair was going on and, of course, they had horses there.

I decided I was going to find that horse and bring it home for a pet. I took a rope and went looking. I showed up at my grandmother's place and told her what I was planning on doing. She wished me luck, gave me some cookies, and sent me on my way.

I walked all over the north side of town. We lived on the south side. I even went across the river to very near the fairgrounds, looking for that horse. Never did find him, but I spent hours looking. I'd never really been around horses. I can't imagine what would have happened had I actually found it. Reality has never really stopped me from trying anything!

I felt very close to my grandmother because she really did care about me, but she left to go work on a newspaper in Idaho when I was maybe second grade.

She told me later that she left mostly to get away from my mother who was driving her nuts. But when she got on that bus and sat by the window waving goodbye to me with tears running down her face, I cried my little heart out. It was one of the few times in my life I remember ever crying. Talk about feeling abandoned! The whole world left me to fend for myself. I still cry for that little girl when I think about that day.

I guess I realized crying wasn't going to have much of a payoff for me. How does a kid that age realize they're never going to see someone again? I knew and I felt totally alone.

She was one of the only ones that even acted like she cared about me, and she was leaving town. She wrote, and sent Easter cookies for a few more years, but it wasn't the same as having her close. I saw her once more when I was seventeen. She was just a cute little old lady in an ankle length dress who smelled like bananas. She had diabetes and wasn't to be around much longer. My then husband and I drove her to Boise to shop, brought her home and never saw her again. She was still wearing Haven's wedding ring and smiled when she talked about him. At least I got to say goodbye.

Chapter 3

My mother boarded me out with a couple for one summer. I don't know where she was or what she was doing, but she sent me to stay with these people. They lived on a farm and they didn't have any children. I was maybe three or four years old. Paul and Paula Paulson were their names. I swear this is true.

They were both very tall. He had to have been over six feet, and she was nearly as tall as he was. I really liked living on their farm. They were very nice to me.

They had pigs. I used to sit and talk to them and feed them Kool-Aid from a little toy bathtub. One day Paula saw me leaning into the pen to retrieve my empty toy bathtub, and she freaked. The pigs were all happily gathered around, oinking and squealing, wanting more grape Kool-Aide.

Paula came running out, long arms flying wildly in the air and snatched me away from the pig pen. Then she gave me a long lecture about how dangerous pigs could be for little girls, and warned me to stay away from them.

I loved the pigs, but I did as I was told and stayed clear of them. The Paulsons were a wonderful couple. They too, wanted to adopt me. I was a cute little kid and behaved pretty well. Who wouldn't want a kid like that?

As soon as they asked my mother about it, she whisked me out of there and that was that. I've never forgotten their kindness toward me. I still have their picture.

The only other relative I had any real knowledge of was my mother's grandmother, her mother's mother. She came to stay with us once for a few months. She was old and was being passed around among the family members. Mom couldn't stand her. She blamed my mother for the death of her daughter, Lura.

It seems Lura, my grandmother, was very sick with the flu during that horrible flu epidemic in the early 1900's. Haven and Bob, my mother's brother, were in the hospital with it. Then my mother, who was maybe four years old, came down with it.

Lura couldn't drive, so she walked the two miles to the hospital carrying her little girl. The young woman was so ill that she died in the hospital within days. She was, maybe, in her very early 20's, and, I recently found out, she was very pregnant.

Her mother felt that somehow it was the fault of that sick little four-year-old girl that she lost her daughter during the epidemic. The old lady lived to be way over a hundred years old, from what my mother told me. She never forgave my mom for "killing" her daughter. My mother was not a popular family member, and that's an understatement.

I was a smart kid and was well able to take care of myself, even as a five- and six-year-old. My mother stopped having baby sitters for me when I was five because she didn't want them eating all her food. The Second World War was just winding down and there wasn't a lot of money. There were trading stamps, used for sugar, flour, coffee, and I don't know what else.

I was left home to fend for myself while she went to work cleaning engines on the railroad. One day I found some of the trading stamps, and when my mother got home, she found them plastered all over the walls and furniture. She screamed, and raged, and cried like a baby over it, and I couldn't figure out what I had done wrong. I was just playing with them. These days, stickers are really popular with kids.

Most the time I did okay taking care of myself. I was very independent and insisted on walking the two miles to kindergarten by myself. I went religiously because they served really good lunches.

My dolls were my best friends. I taught them to read and I had some of the smartest dolls in the world! I wasn't allowed to play with other kids much, so I spent way too much time alone. This really stunted my social abilities.

The mind gets morbid when it's left to its own devises too much. I took to killing ants and having elaborate funerals in the back yard for them. I'm not sure how I knew how a funeral went, let alone what they were. I knew they had to do with dead things.

I remember once, my mother and I were in a funeral parlor. I think my mother was cleaning it at the time. There was a body in a casket waiting for his funeral. I walked up to the casket, looked at the body, and decided I wanted to touch it. I reached into the casket, put my hand close to his face, and I swear I saw him blink. I freaked and ran like a scared rabbit to find my mother. Maybe that's where I learned about funerals.

I later, as a first and second grader, would leave school, and go home to play school with my dolls. The real school bored me. I was profoundly hard of hearing, but nobody caught on. I was always seated at the back of the room, and couldn't hear what was being said.

At home alone, I'd turn the radio up full blast and listen to opera. I loved the operatic music and, incredibly, sort of understood what was going on. I couldn't listen to it when my mother was there. She didn't like the "noise". I loved the tenors especially, and still do. Their voices soothed me, somehow.

As I said earlier, my mother worked at the roundhouse across the river, cleaning train engines during the war. She was always adamant that I didn't say anything about the epilepsy. Back then, people with epilepsy were considered crazy and dangerous, and had a lot of trouble finding work. The seizures were referred to as "fits" and people didn't rush to help if they saw one. They walked the other way or stood and stared.

Mom seemed to relate to me as a buddy, or non-existent, never as a daughter. If there was a man in her life she saw me as competition. She would come home from work and tell me the latest dirty joke she'd heard that day. The scary part was that I actually understood some of them.

One day, she came home and told me she'd nearly fallen into

the Missouri River. She rode her bicycle everywhere. At age four, I graduated from the basket to the fender. I soon was begging for a bike of my own. Wanting some dignity, I guess. I got one after I proved to her I could ride her adult bike. I nearly killed myself on it, and got yelled at when I crashed it a couple of times, but I earned my own kid's bike.

Anyhow, she had to ride across a train trestle with a walkway to one side of the tracks, to get across the river to and from work. There was a huge hole on the walkway, and when she tried to ride around it she lost control. The front of the bike went through the hole with her hanging onto the handle bars. Luckily, the back wheel turned and caught the bike preventing it from going into the river.

Mom hung there over the river for several minutes. It probably seemed like hours. She said she hollered her head off. Some guys came along and pulled her and the bike out of the hole.

The thing of it was, she was hanging there using only her right hand, because her partially paralyzed left hand was useless. This woman was nothing if not strong.

I didn't have a lot of experience with death, so it didn't scare me all that much. I didn't relate to the possibility of my mother dying. I just thought it was kind of a neat story. It amazes me now that she was able to hang on like that with only one good hand.

Separation anxiety was never an issue for me. I was used to being alone because I spent most of my time that way. I wasn't really bonded to anyone except maybe my grandmother and I learned she couldn't be trusted.

The only real experience I had, with the death of someone I knew, was an old man that my mother worked for when I was three or four. He had been a friend of my grandfather Haven, and he either owned a steamship line, or booked passage on them. Mom answered phones in his office and cleaned his rental houses for him. I think if he'd been younger, he would have married her, probably out of pity, and a sense of loyalty to my grandfather.

My mother would take me to work with her and he would take me to the corner drug store and buy me a root beer float. I was home alone one day when she called out of the blue to tell me he had died. Hell, I didn't even know he was sick. I cried for a long time, not grieving his death, but grieving the root beer floats. I really believed

I would never get another one. I'm not sure how I understood that he was gone, but I didn't have another root beer float until way into my thirties.

I finally realized I was connecting the float to the old man, and the little girl in me still thought he was the only source of root beer floats. I wonder how many people are hampered by beliefs developed in childhood and never explored as adults. Probably, most of us are.

There was a movie theater around the corner from my root beer float benefactor's office. I found that I could go upstairs in the building next door, and sneak into the balcony of the theater.

Theaters were beautifully ornate back then, with wood carvings on the walls, and deep purple velveteen curtains framing the stage where the movie screen was located. The balconies were high above the main floor, and could be hung over to watch the people below watching the movie.

Sometimes, it was fun to rain popcorn down on the audience below, then watch as the ushers came running, trying to catch the culprit who caused the storm. Of course, far be it from me to do something like that!

I would go clear to the top of the balcony, up against the wall, and watch movies over and over again, for hours. My favorite was, "The Red Pony". I think I watched that movie seven times. I would cry over the dead pony, sitting there sobbing, tears pouring down my face as the little boy held his soaked pony, and watched it die of pneumonia. It was the only crying I allowed myself to do. I still love that movie.

I loved the westerns too and I spent a lot of time trying to figure out how those cowboys could get shot, die, and come back to do the show all over again.

When I wasn't watching movies, I was digging through the garbage in the back of the Safeway store that was close by and eating discarded lettuce, and other vegetables. I know my mother fed me sometimes and I'm not sure why I was eating out of the dumpster.

I always had a thing about food and still do. I have to have lots of food around me all the time. I don't have to eat it, just know it's there. I finally quit carrying fruit in my purse. When it starts to overripen it can get pretty messy!

I think, because my mother made such an issue out of it, food became an obsession for me. She'd gone through the great depression and that was probably why it was an issue for her. I don't think her parents ever had problems feeding their kids. Fear runs down hill.

After the old man died, we didn't go to the office any more. That's when I started killing ants and other bugs, and having elaborate funerals for them. I wasn't taken to his funeral, but I knew how funerals worked. I would pray over those insects and solemnly bury them in the back yard. I had a special hole I used for all of them.

I'm not sure how I found out about God either. I seem to remember saying prayers with my grandmother when I was very small. The "now I lay me down to sleep" version was my nightly prayer.

Dogs and cats weren't allowed in the housing project we lived in, so I couldn't even have a real pet. Some people sneaked them in, but my mother tried to obey the rules. The only pets I was allowed to have were turtles. I had two of them, both of which died, and had wonderful funerals. At least, I think they died. I found out later that turtles hibernate. I sure hope that wasn't the case with those two!

Once, when I was maybe five or six, my mother and I were in a pet shop downtown. It must have been around Easter, because they had bunnies. I actually talked my mother into buying one of them. I guess she was feeling motherly, or trying to save face with the sales person. Anyhow, we brought it home and she immediately took it to a friend of hers that kept rabbits.

Maybe a month or so later, we went to the woman's house for dinner. I walked around her pens looking for my rabbit, and didn't see it. At dinner I asked her where it was. My mother's friend said, and I am not making this up, "You're eating it. It couldn't have babies, so I butchered it."

People back then really didn't realize that children were human too and had human feelings.   I didn't finish that dinner, and I never ate rabbit again. I was sick and sad for weeks.

In my desperation for company and a pet I would pick up stray cats and bring them home. I'd play with them, then hide them in the closet before my mother got home. They'd howl and yowl, and my mother would come home and discover them.

She'd take them outside, and throw them over the roof of the complex we lived in. One small kitten she dropped into a dug-out basement on the way to walking me to kindergarten. My crying and begging didn't make any difference. It just pissed her off. I think this incident is what made me decide to walk myself to school from then on.

I finally gave up on the cats. I had a stuffed dog about the size of a cocker spaniel. He was white and fluffy and I wanted him to be real. I'd put him in my doll bed at night, and pray that he'd become a real dog by morning. I was big on God and what he might do for me. He just wasn't willing to turn a stuffed dog into a real one. The way my mother treated animals, I guess that was a blessing.

I've made up for it as an adult. I keep lots of animals around me. It's a wonder that I had any empathy for animals after growing up watching the way she treated them.

Chapter 4

I was scared to death of my mother. She loomed as a bit of a monster in my mind. I really wasn't conscious of how I perceived her until way into my adulthood. I guess I was so caught up in self-protection that I never allowed the feelings to surface.

She sat at the big roll-top desk in the root beer float guy's office one day, while she was working, and pulled the legs off a cockroach. She'd laugh when the strange bug skittered around on its belly, helplessly lifting its wings as if to try to fly, trying to get away from her, while her little four-year-old sat watching in horror. I honestly thought, if I defied her, she could do that to me too.

I learned real quickly not to let this strange woman mess with my hair. As I said earlier, she was crippled on the left side and had trouble using her left hand. When she would try to put pin curls in my hair, she'd fumble around, getting so frustrated she'd slap me upside the head. I learned to do my own hair at a very young age, and soon, I was doing hers too. I really didn't want her to be "motherly". It was too unsettling.

I dreaded the epileptic seizures. We lived in a one-bedroom

unit in the housing development, and I slept in her bed with her. Mom had grand mal seizures, and, sometimes in the night, she'd wake me up screaming and foaming at the mouth like she was possessed.

One night, she managed to get a hold on my wrist with her right hand and nearly broke it before I could get loose. I was so grateful when she got married and I got my own bed.

One spring day we were downtown shopping and she fell into a seizure while we were crossing Central Avenue, the main street in Great Falls. I was probably seven or eight and not very big, but I literally pulled her bodily off the street to keep her from being run down.   Nobody stopped to try and help. This didn't scare me exactly. It just made me very watchful and made me feel responsible for her.

I was taught by her that the seizures were shameful and were to be kept a secret, no matter what. One day she was standing talking to one of her friends through the front door screen and she started going into one of her seizures. I slammed the door in the woman's face so she wouldn't see what was going on. Having epilepsy was something to hide and be ashamed of back then.

Her grand mal motor seizures were especially frightening. She would scream, run and fall, curl into an embryonic ball and foam at the mouth, all the time screaming in a low guttural tone. Then, when she came out of it, she'd look confused and ask what just happened.

When I was old enough, mom would tell me stories about herself and her husbands. I was four or five when she told me about my father and his burglarizing and how their marriage ended.

She told me a story of being in a bus station, after Harry, her second husband, disappeared. She was changing my diaper and the Red Cross came in, wanting to know if they could help. I guess I was crying pretty hard. I think about it now and realize she was probably spanking me, trying to get me to shut up and someone got concerned. She didn't have good frustration control.

She told me about being so hungry while working in the cotton fields, that one night, one of the farmer's roosters wandered by the hut she was living in. She said she grabbed it, wrung its neck and cooked it. Again, I had another reason to fear her. I could see that poor rooster so vividly and, of course, I related to what she might do to me if she got mad or hungry enough. You've gotta be careful what you tell little kids.

During all of this, she had me boarded out with someone. When she got me back, she said I was covered with boils. I guess they'd been feeding me goat's milk and I was allergic to it. So, back we went, to Great Falls, and my mother continued on her impulsive ways.

She was married twice more while we lived in Parkdale. Once to a drunk, who thought he'd like to try out a naïve little girl. I was four, and he invited me into his bed one morning when I was playing nurse with him. He worked nights in a tavern, she worked days. Even then, being raised with no real guidance, my instincts about people were good. When he invited me to climb into bed with him, I shouted no and I left the bedroom. That was the end of that.

She kicked him out when he came home drunk one night. He broke a wine bottle on the front porch before he left, screaming profanities at her.

We lived alone, in our crazy weird little world, for a while after that. Mom was a good housekeeper back then. She had some nice furniture, that, I think she had bought herself. She told me that when I was maybe three years old, I took a razor blade to the coffee table when she wasn't there. From then on, I was forbidden to sit on the furniture.

I didn't remember doing that, but it wouldn't surprise me. I do remember hating that furniture. I felt that it was a lot more important to her than I was. I probably wasn't far off.

She would sit on the blue sofa, and I'd play on the floor with a little toy village I had. The radio would be on and we'd listen to the wonderful programs; "Our Miss Brooks", "Baby Snooks", "The Shadow" and "Amos and Andy". On Saturday morning, I never missed "Let's Pretend", a show that acted out fairy tales. The sponsor was "Cream of Wheat" and I still remember the jingle. I lived for that show, and I ate Cream of Wheat religiously while I listened. Those were some of the fond memories of my childhood.

My mother started locking me out of the house when I was about six or seven. A little girl from across the walk, who was older than me, decided one day that we should make fudge. Because my mother wasn't home, we girls decided to do it in my mother's kitchen.

The whole kitchen became a chocolate-covered disaster and the girl and I moved the project to her house. This meant a pan, dripping chocolate, was carried across my mother's perfect back yard lawn and over the fence she had built around the yard. The chocolate path led to the girl's kitchen across the walk.

All I remember about the incident was dreading my mother coming home, and the fit she threw when she saw the mess we'd made. From then on, locked out of the house, I waited in the back yard until she got home, summer and winter.

My mother had friends, but, as I said before, I didn't have much interaction with other kids.

There was a little girl whose mother played the piano. My mother would take me with her when she went to visit. Glenda and I would play, and listen to her mom's music. That's probably where I developed my love for the piano.

Glenda was a rather mean, spoiled little kid. One day she and I sat on a curb on the main road going past Parkdale, and threw rocks at cars going by. Suddenly, a woman pulled her car over, came flying out of it and chased us down. She ran past me, swatting me on the butt as she flew by, and, when I caught up with her and Glenda, the woman was sitting on a bench, she had Glenda bent over her lap, and was spanking her. Glenda was screaming and I just kept on running. That was probably the first and only spanking that kid ever got.

I can't speak for Glenda, but that incident sure scared me straight. I never threw rocks at cars again. The woman turned out to be the mother of the little girl of the fudge incident.

One night, my mother and Glenda's dad went out to get a bottle and my mother was very drunk when they came back. Glenda and I came into the kitchen and my mom was sitting in a corner on the floor crying. She said Glenda's dad made her drink the booze. Glenda's dad stood staring at her looking a bit stunned. Somehow we got back to our house and I don't remember ever seeing Glenda or her folks again until I was much older.

There was an old lady who lived two doors down from Glenda. I would go to her house to visit, and she'd teach me how to knit round pillows. She gave me a box of chocolate cherries one day, I don't remember the occasion, but I remember I ate the whole box and became violently ill. To this day, I can't look a chocolate-covered cherry in the face.

Chapter 5

My mother had a friend, Mildred, who lived in one of the two-story units with a drunken husband and three kids. One day my mother was visiting her. Her kids spirited me out of the house and took me into the crawl space under the huge building. It was very dark. I was maybe five or six at the time.

They sat me down across from a girl dressed up like a fortune teller. She told my fortune using cards. Then, suddenly, all the kids got up and took off, locking me under the building. It was pitch black and I couldn't see a thing, except for a little light around the opening in the crawl space. I beat frantically on the little door, and the kids kept yelling at me from the other side to be careful of the spiders and the ghosts.

I screamed, and cried, and begged to be let out. I was terrified.

They finally let me out and called me a chicken and a cry-baby.

I had horrible nightmares after that and would wake up thinking spiders were crawling on me. I could feel my body smashing them as I tossed, and rolled, and screamed. My mother would get angry and yell at me because I woke her up and she had to go to work the next morning. I still have bad claustrophobia from that incident.

For some reason, once in a while my mother and Mildred would get into fights. Mildred was very short like my mother and weighed about the same, so they were fairly evenly matched, although my mother had that treacherous right hand.

I remember one day being on the bus with my mother, coming from downtown. I must have been seven or eight years old. Mildred was on the bus also, and they were mad at each other. My mother told me she was going to catch Mildred and beat her up. I tried in vain to talk her out of it, but we breezed past our stop.

I followed mom off the bus when Mildred got off at her stop. I was trying to talk her out of doing what she planned to do.

I swear to God, I couldn't believe it. My mother went limping after the woman, who was walking as fast as she could to get away. I was astonished that Mildred was actually scared. They wound up in a fist fight, with me trying to get them to stop. I wasn't a crier, so I shouted and ran around the screaming, punching tangle of women, until another adult came along and pulled them apart.

These were women in their early thirties, acting like thugs. The next time they were together, it was like nothing had ever happened. They were buddies again.   I never understood these women.   It was the weirdest thing.

One Halloween night, my mother, Mildred, and another woman friend of theirs went out in full costume, and stole candy from kids that were trick-or-treating. Then they went to a fourth friend's house and had coffee and donuts. All of them laughed about it, acting as if this was normal behavior for grown women.

My mother told me all about it when she got home. She also told me not to ever tell anyone.   Now I'm telling anyone who reads this!   In the meantime, while those wild and crazy women were terrorizing the kids in Parkdale, I went out alone and got my own candy the right way. While I was out, I ran into someone dressed like a ghost, and, thinking it was my mother, I went up to it and said, "Mom?" It was another kid, and they told me to get lost and walked away. Boy, did I feel silly.

Later that night, some kids tried to raid the neighbor's garden across the walk from us. I stood there watching them, contemplating if I should go over the fence and join them. They were giggling and laughing as they picked her vegetables.

Her parrot, perched in a swing on the porch, went nuts and started yelling at them. He squawked, "Kids in the garden" over and over. They freaked out and ran, stumbling over the woman's fence holding bunches of carrots and corn. I was nearly knocked down while they attempted their getaway, the old woman screaming profanities at them as they ran. I almost got blamed for that one, but I escaped back into my house just in time.

Chapter 6

I went to school, from nursery school to fourth grade, living in that project in a one- bedroom unit. I had a little boyfriend, Robert, who lived a couple of rows down from us. When I'd take one of my dolls to school, he'd carry it home for me, with kids following along behind, teasing him. He didn't seem to care.

His mother made him stop playing with me because I tried to get him to skip school one day and stay home with me. He did stay for a few minutes, then got so scared he left, making a run for the school, hoping not to be too late. We were second or third graders at the time. He was probably the only black kid that lived in Great Falls back then. I hope he grew up and married somebody wonderful. He was a good kid and truly thought I was wonderful.

I skipped school a lot, or I would go to school, and leave, probably partially because of my lack of hearing. I'd say I had to go to the bathroom and I'd leave the school and sneak onto the city bus. I'd ride downtown and wander around the stores.

Sneaking on the bus was a piece of cake. You just took hold of an adult's coat and the driver thought you were with them. Kids rode free with an adult. It seems strange to me today that the school never reported me missing, no search was done, nothing.

Sometimes I'd steal little figurines from the dime store to take home to my mother. When the J.C. Penney's store got the first escalator in Great Falls, I loved running down the up and up the down, and would spend hours dodging people to play on the weird moving stairs. I never got kicked out of the store. I think they thought I belonged to someone.

One Christmas, I was probably seven or eight years old, I decided to visit the Penney's Santa Claus. When it was my turn, I got on his lap and started to tell him what I wanted for Christmas. I noticed his beard didn't fit quite right and I said so. Before he could shove me off his lap I got hold of the beard, and gave it a tug. It came off in my hand. I was horrified and so was Santa, as well as the other kids waiting to talk to him.

He jumped up, dumping me on the floor, and ducked behind his throne. A store clerk came running and wanted to know where my mother was. I had gotten up off the floor, and, realizing I was in trouble, I ran for the escalator with the clerk in hot pursuit. I managed to run down the escalator and out the door before he caught up with me. Jeez, you'd think I was caught shoplifting, or something.   I thought the whole thing was pretty funny, but had nobody to tell about it until now.

Nobody at school ever questioned where I was or why I was gone. I was a pain for the teachers, I think. I talked all the time. I remember a first grade teacher putting tape over my mouth to shut me up. I spent the rest of the day goofing off by licking on the tape to try to get it off. I think the teachers were kind of glad to not have to deal with me when I'd leave. I dealt with my humiliation by goofing off and trying to be silly.

My mother showed up in the classroom a couple of times when I was in first or second grade, but she never had an explanation as to what she was doing there. The teachers were probably complaining about my behavior. I thought it was kind of neat that she'd come to my school and watch. Maybe she did have some interest in me, or she was afraid of losing her babysitting if they kicked me out.

The only spanking I ever remember getting from my mother was with a hair brush when I was seven. I had come home from downtown and brought her some glass figurines I'd stolen from Kress's, which was the dime store. I told her I found them. I'm not sure, but I think she spanked me for leaving school. She wanted me to cry, but, even then, there was no way I'd give her that kind of satisfaction. I just stood there and let her hit me until her arm got tired and she gave up.

Her friend Mildred was there and when I think about the

incident now, my mother might have been performing for her. Mom was a hitter when she got frustrated, but not a spanker.

My mother wasn't always oblivious to me. She played with me sometimes. We'd hike, or ride bikes, and play stick ball. I threw up on her once when we were in a park downtown, and she was pushing me on a swing. I warned her I was getting sick, but she just kept pushing. She was pretty quiet on the way home that day, probably because of a sore throat from cussing me out for making a mess on her.

She didn't have a whole lot of sense at times. We were walking along some railroad tracks and a train came from around a bend. She was just oblivious to it. I jumped off the tracks, yelling at her as I did. She ignored me till the very last minute, then looked shocked to see the train and got off the tracks in time. It scared hell out of me.

She met a guy, Joe, when I was nine. He was one of the few sober working men she ever married. He was from Canada, in his forties, and he had worked as a farm hand most of his life. In his early years he'd worked in coal mines and had what they called, "black lung" from the experience. He even had coal dust under the skin of his arms. He only made it through third grade before he went to work in the mines.

The way she caught him was she told him she was pregnant. Being an honorable man, he married her, paid off all her bills, moved us into a two-story unit in Parkdale, and I got my first bedroom. This was his first, and probably last, marriage. He was really angry about being duped like that. No, she wasn't pregnant, and he wasn't in love with her. He was actually in love with her friend who had killed my pet rabbit and tried to feed it to me.

I was so thrilled to have a room of my own, that I slept on the floor that first night. Joe, apparently, was so touched by that, he went out and bought me a bed and a dresser the next day. I was in heaven. We lived in that unit for about six months, then the moving around began.

While we were living there, a beautiful little black cocker spaniel followed me home from school one day. He hung around at night and walked me to school in the morning. I really wanted to keep that little dog, and begged my mother to let me have him.

He disappeared after a few days. My mother told me she took him over on the north side of town and left him. I went over there two days in a row and walked for miles, rope in my hand, calling and hoping to find him. Never did, of course. I cried my heart out over him as I walked. It was a sad time for me. My mother later told me she'd taken him to the pound. Her cruelty and thoughtlessness just knew no bounds.

I don't know when Joe found out that my mother had lied to him, and she wasn't pregnant, but he developed a hatred for her that was visible. I only experienced
one of the beatings he gave her, but I know he slapped her around a lot.

I was oblivious to most of it because he didn't normally get physical with her when I was around. He had some interesting values around kids and how to treat them. Joe was the only husband, out of the nine she had, that acknowledged my existence. He seemed to like me a lot and was a decent father for a lonely little step-kid.

I came home from school one day when we lived in Fort Benton, and my mother had a bad burn on her lip. She told me he had taken a cigarette and tried to shove the lit end into her mouth. He didn't like her smoking. It was the financial part he didn't like. He was very tight with his money and hers. He also had broken her glasses, hitting her in the face. So, from then on, if he was going to beat her up, he'd remove her glasses.

He bought a little house in Fort Benton, and moved us there, after several moves around the state working on different farms. He drove a little Jeep, and I loved riding in the back of it. I had never experienced love for anyone but my grandmother, but I liked this guy.

He really tried to be a good father to me and didn't take his hatred for my mother out on me. He loved to play Canasta with me because I could beat him every time. He was fascinated by that and we'd play for hours. I'm sure my mother was very jealous, but she never said anything.

As I said, Joe was a farm hand, so he and my mother would go work on farms. She would cook, and he would work as a farm hand. Usually, they would board me out to strangers in town so I could go to school.

I think he knew I was lonely, and after two cats dying of distemper, he let me have a little half Cocker, half Scottie puppy. I kept that pup with me all the time, even taking it to bed with me. I called her Trixie. She peed the bed one night and I told the lady I was boarded with at the time that I had done it. She knew better and wouldn't let me sleep with the pup any more.

One day, in school, Trixie showed up in my classroom. To this day, I don't know how she got there. I just remember crying and sobbing and freaking out, thinking I was going
to lose my puppy. The teacher didn't get it. Nobody got it with me. He said, rather cruelly I thought, "What are you bawling about? Just take the puppy home."

I did, and my mother and Joe took it with them out to the farm they were working on. From then on the dog became my mother's pet.

Joe asked me one day if I wanted to learn to play an instrument. His boss's daughter played one and he wanted me to have the same experience. I got very excited and said yes. I tried to describe a clarinet to him. He came home with a beautiful silver

Bundy flute. At first I was disappointed, but I learned to play it quickly, and I loved it. I spent hours playing that thing, but the joy only lasted a few months.

One Saturday afternoon, a fight erupted in the house. My mother had made pancake batter, planning on pancakes for breakfast. She cooked on an old wood stove and it was very hot. She had left a light on in the bedroom, or some stupid thing.

Joe was always complaining about using too much electricity and he even got upset if she vacuumed too long. Anyway, he started yelling at her. She got angry, started swearing at him and doused him with the pancake batter. The fight was on.

I panicked, and ran out to the coal shed with Trixie. We hunkered down and listened to the screaming. It got so loud and frightening that I thought he was killing her. I tried to run back into the house to stop it. Joe saw me coming and slammed the door before I could reach the house. I ran the two blocks to the town police station to try and get help.

Believe it or not, they told me my mother would have to come in and file charges. I stared at them in disbelief.

"She can't come in," I screamed at them. "He's beating her up."

The cop said, shrugging his shoulders, "Well, we can't do anything until she comes in, and files charges against him. She'll have to divorce him too."

I was stunned. I ran back to the house, went back into the coal shed and held tight to the dog as we listened to my mother still screaming.

Finally, she came running out of the house. Her face was a mess and she had a severe burn down her right arm. She had picked up the skillet with hot grease in it and tried to throw it at Joe. The wooden handle had turned and the scalding grease poured down her arm, melting skin, and the fat under it.

I walked her up to the hospital, talking all the way, trying to convince her that she needed to divorce this guy before he killed her. I was maybe eleven years old.

She did listen to me and divorced him. She never forgave me for talking her into it, although I'm sure Joe would have given me a medal for convincing her to leave him. I think the only reason he stayed as long as he did was he didn't want to lose any of the "stuff" they'd accumulated. Joe wound up in jail and my mother was on to a new guy.

Chapter 7

We found ourselves on a train ride to Butte, Montana, along with Mildred's drunken ex-husband, another Joe. We moved into a hotel room there, and he stayed drunk the whole time. My mother left me with him and went back to Fort Benton to settle with Joe the farm hand.

The only possession I got to keep was a blue teddy bear that I kept with me until I was 21 years old. Everything else, including the flute, was gone. I accepted the losses like I did all losses. I moved on and didn't look back.

I spent the whole three days she was gone playing fantasy games under the covers in my bed, eating soda crackers and water, and wandering around town. There was a beautiful Sonia Heinie doll in a store window that I spent a lot of time staring at while my mother was gone. Joe just stayed drunk.

When she came back, she bought me the Sonia doll, figure skates and all, probably out of guilt for getting rid of everything I owned. To this day I don't know what happened to that doll, but I thought she was the most beautiful thing in the world.

Joe, the drunk, my mother, and I, headed for Seattle. Why they decided to go there, I don't know. I was just part of the baggage and never consulted about anything.

We moved into an Airstream camp trailer in a trailer park. My mother finally got sick of Joe's drinking and kicked him out. She spent her time cleaning the trailer court manager's house, and fooling around with the woman's husband.

I went to school sometimes, but spent most of my time hanging out around the trailer court. I used to go to the manager's house when my mother was there and load up on canned goods. We never seemed to have any money or food in the trailer. I think my mother was able to get away with this in trade for whatever, from the manager's husband.

I experienced my first sexual molestation in this trailer court. I was still only eleven years old. A huge heavy-set guy called Tiny used to like to get me into his car parked near the SeaTac runways. We'd watch the planes take off and land and he'd have his hand down my panties. Strangely, it was a turn-off, but at least I was being touched, talked to, and getting attention. I never related to any of it as "right or wrong". It was just uncomfortable.

Tiny never tried to actually have sex with me. Oh, he offered if I ever wanted to, but he wasn't aggressive. The guy was every bit as screwed up as I was, and to this day, I don't have any real resentment toward him and never did. I feel badly for other lonely little girls he probably got to, though.

We moved into a housing project and my mother met some guy. She actually tried to hook me up with the man's friend. She was not quite forty years old and these guys were close to her age. I went out with the guy a couple of times. He took me to the Crystal Mountain ski lodge near Mount Rainier once. We drank and danced, and went to a cabin he had rented. I was a very mature-looking twelve-year-old. He didn't do anything sexual at the cabin, because he passed out. The next morning he took me home.

The third time he came I hid in a closet and told her to tell him I wasn't there. He brought me nylons as a gift. I had enough sense to be disgusted by him. He never came back, and she stayed mad at me for a while over it. I think she really had it in her head that, if she could find a guy to take me on, he'd support her too.

I was in seventh grade by then. My mother was gone a lot and I skipped school a lot. I failed the grade and really didn't want to go back to school. That period of time is a bit of a blur. I remember going to a neighborhood bakery and the owner would give me day-old donuts. I'd take them home. Sometimes, that's all we had to eat that day. I'm sure my mother was struggling with depression and so was I.

One summer, while in Washington, my mother and I spent the season picking strawberries on a farm. We lived, along with other migrant workers, in a large barn that had been converted into a dormitory.

There was a small grocery store on the place that gave credit to the workers. My mother and I would charge food there and when we'd get paid, the debt would get taken out of the picking money. Usually, the debt was nearly equal to the money we made, so we would get maybe a dollar or two for the week. I didn't make much money, picking strawberries. I had a deep love for the fruit, and tended to eat most of what I picked.

The neighbor next door in Parkdale had a garden and grew his strawberries next to our fence. I practically lived on his fruit as a little girl.

One day my mother and I were walking down the dirt road that led to the little store. I picked up a pretty good-sized King snake on the road and scared the hell out of her with it, chasing her around.

I took it back to the dormitory and put it in one of the girls' bed. Then I crawled into my bed and waited for the reaction. She gave me a good one. I've never heard anyone scream like that.

The scary part, looking back on that incident, is that it could have just as easily been a rattlesnake and I wouldn't have known the difference. All of us were lucky that day.

I spent a lot of time downtown on the streets of Seattle, when we lived there, running around with other feral kids that no one cared about. I was just wandering through life, with no identity and no way of knowing, or even caring, about what would come next.

I was angry, lonely, and had no social skills. I didn't like people, thought adults were stupid, and really wasn't sure I liked myself. I had no real concept of my own existence. So I just wandered and waited for the next move to be made. I had no concept of how normal people lived. I just lived in the moment, and, believe me, that way of being is really not all that people seem to think it is. There was no past, no future, just waiting for the next moment to happen, and reacting to it.

My mother moved to Havre, Montana, with me in tow, when I turned thirteen. Why Havre, I have no idea. Her whimsical ways have always been a mystery to me.

I took up smoking by the time I was twelve years old. I had tried it when we lived in Fort Benton, with Joe, the farm hand. A kid saw me smoking behind a piece of farm machinery next door to my house and started teasing me.

One day I was walking down the street with Joe when the kid walked by and said, "Hey, Smokey". Joe looked at me funny and I never tried smoking again while we were with him. I saw what he did to my mother for smoking. I wasn't going to set myself up for that.

My mother caught me smoking one day, while we were still in the projects in Seattle. She brought home a cigar and said, "If you can smoke this, then you can smoke cigarettes." She finally made me put the thing out when I was halfway through it, because the cigar smoke stunk so badly. I smoked cigarettes from then on.

When we got to Havre, the cigarette had become an important part of my tough persona. It was the early fifties, and my identity became the tough street kid in jeans and flannel shirt with a cigarette hanging out of the corner of her mouth.

I partnered up with a big strong girl named Patty. She was the "gentle giant" type, and loved riding horses. She knew an old guy who had a riding stable just outside town. When he was gone we'd go there, saddle a couple of horses, and go riding. Usually, we'd get them back before he came home. I took to going there alone and taking a gentle paint to ride, when he was gone.

One day, I couldn't get the horse to go past a piece of equipment parked along a curb in town. My anger flared and I beat that poor horse unmercifully with a belt buckle, putting marks on her butt. She just stood and took it. I finally got off and led her past the machine. Even writing this brings tears and makes me feel guilt over that incident. I just was so angry and lost I took it out on everything, even the innocent.

Patty, the giant, and I hung out in a local soda shop with other teens and acted tough. Most of the kids were afraid of us. We'd pick someone out and I'd pick a fight with them. My big friend would step in and finish it. Patty wasn't particularly temperamental, she just liked to fight. We thought this was great fun until one day we picked the wrong girl.

She was a little oriental girl with ridiculously long fingernails, waist-long black hair, and a mean streak. She had a penchant for wanting to fight as well, and even though she was small, she was tough, and she knew how to use those claws.

I called her out one day in the soda shop and when Patty

stepped in to finish it, the girl raked her across the face with her fingernails. Patty became enraged. I'd never seen her like that before. She lifted the tiny teen-ager up over her head and threw her through the plate-glass window.

There was a huge ruckus, cops and all. I got the hell out of there and I never saw Patty or the little oriental girl again. Nor did I even wonder about them. People and things just came and went in my life and I didn't ask questions.

I ran around with my thumbs hooked in the waist of my jeans and a cigarette hanging out of the corner of my mouth. I dared anyone to challenge me. Once, in the town movie theater, a boy got smart with me and I, without even batting an eye, kicked him hard between the legs. It never dawned on me that I could have done serious damage to him. I'm not sure I would have cared if I had. I just turned and walked away, leaving him on the floor crying, and went to watch the movie.

I met a little Native American girl around my age. Her name was Sherry. She lived with her grandmother and grandfather. They didn't have much use for me. I think they knew I was trouble.

Sherry too, was somewhat of a lost soul. Most of our relationship was spent running away from home. She was unhappy with her grandparents. I just did it for a lark. I had no place to run from or to.

One night we found ourselves with a really nasty guy. He'd pulled a "put out or walk" on me. I'd got out of the car to walk, but we were so far out and it was dark, so I got back into the car. For some reason, he changed his mind and took us back to town.

I don't remember how Sherry and I hooked up with this freak again. He'd bought a bottle of slow gin, and we were invited to share it with him. We were having a gay old time getting drunk until the guy decided he wanted to play with the little virgin. I was so drunk all I could do was comfort her while he raped her. I didn't relate to it as rape.

She cried and I cried, and mercifully, he finally dropped us off in the middle of town and we found our way home. I had lost my virginity to this guy earlier, before I met Sherry. It sickens me today just to think about that situation. Some men really took advantage of kids like us that didn't know what was okay, and what wasn't. Thank God today, women are speaking out and teaching girls what's okay and what's not,

concerning what men do.

I'll never forget my first period, though. I'm not sure how I knew what it was, but I was sure excited. I didn't tell anyone, not even my mother. I just took one of her Kotex and took care of it. All I could think of was, "now I could have babies. I could have little people of my own to love and they would love me back. I wouldn't be alone any more".

Thank God, or whoever was watching over me that that didn't happen then. It would have been a disaster for me and the kid.

Chapter 8

Sherry and I got into all sorts of trouble together. One time we hid out in an empty house that belonged to her uncle, for several days. My mother was living in a little camp trailer near downtown at the time. I was never home so she didn't bother worrying about where I might sleep in that little trailer. Sherry and I visited the trailer a couple of times, when my mother wasn't there, and stole food from her. My mother tried to tie the door closed with apron strings. I thought that was pretty funny as I yanked on the door and tore the apron in half. I later found out she thought street people were coming in and stealing from her. I guess in a way, they were.

The family next door to the house Sherry and I were hiding in had a beautiful garden. They grew delicious corn. We girls would pick it and eat it raw. Neither one of us knew how to cook. One day, the neighbor showed up at the door and accused us of taking his corn. We, of course, denied it with corn juice dripping down our faces, and corn leaves scattered all over the kitchen floor.

He left and the next thing we knew, there was another knock on the door. This time, it was Sharon's uncle and the Sheriff.

Sharon dove behind the couch and told me not to tell her uncle she was there. We were both young teen-agers and really not thinking straight.

I did what she asked. However, her feet were sticking out from the back of the couch. Her uncle grabbed her by the heels and yanked her out. The Sheriff laughed his head off over that. Sherry got to her feet and both of us were taken home. By then my mother was living in a motel in town.

Three days later, Sherry and I hooked up again and took off hitchhiking for Great Falls. It was about 150 miles or so, away. She had stolen her aunt's glasses and I had a pair of high heels that I'd gotten from somewhere. We traded off throughout the trip, thinking we were disguising ourselves. Our ultimate goal was New York City.
Remember, we were only 13 years old and loaded with adventurism.

We got several rides and nobody tried to harm us, or question why two thirteen-year- old girls were hitchhiking across Montana.

When we got to Great Falls, we stole some hair dye and spent the afternoon in a gas station bathroom dying my hair red. It came out a beautiful orange color because we didn't read the directions and just rubbed the stuff dry into my hair; then rinsed it out. I was lucky my hair didn't fall out.

Sherry wanted to look up her mother, so we did. The young teen was the last person her mother wanted to see. She gave Sherry some money and sent us on our way. We hitched a couple of rides and landed in Helena, the state Capital. That's where my uncle Bob lived. He worked for the local newspaper and his wife worked for the state.

I called him and he came and got us. I told him we were going to hitchhike to New York. No small goals for us girls!

Bob and his wife cleaned us up and fed us. Then my uncle, unceremoniously, took us to the bus station and bought tickets back to Havre.

We had managed to steal two cartons of cigarettes from a store after he dropped us off, so Sherry and I spent the all-night trip on the bus singing loudly, and scattering cigarettes around the long back seat. We must have driven the other passengers nuts, but no one said a word to us. I'm sure the bus driver breathed a sigh of relief when we got off in Havre.

Sherry and I also had an experience with a couple of rodeo riders, a bottle of vodka, and a motel. The cowboy I was with walked me around and around the building, trying to
sober me up. He never once tried to get into my pants, or even try to kiss me. He seemed more concerned that I was physically okay. He was really a very nice guy and I hope he has had a wonderful life;

Sharon was inside with her cowboy, necking. This was the last time I saw her, until we both wound up in the reform school.

I met Ron through another girl I was running with. I was thirteen. He had said he was 21, but I later found out he was closer to 25 at the time. He worked for the railroad, had been married once, and had a two-year-old daughter who lived with his parents in Bozeman.

We were still living in the motel when I met Ron. I realize now he was a sexual predator and liked messing around with young girls. At that time I thought he was my savior.

He had a brand new 1954 Dodge and he taught me to drive it. I was still only 13, but he had me driving him all over town. One morning he decided to let me have his car for the day. Did I mention he was a very immature and a rather stupid twenty-five?

Boy, did I have fun with that car. I took off and drove to Great Falls with it. On the way I got caught between two semi-trucks driving across an overpass. A semi was coming toward me, also. I panicked, and got too close to the barrier and side swiped the car. I managed to get control again and happily went on my way.

When I got to Great Falls I stopped to pick up an old girl friend from years ago. She was the daughter of the rabbit lady. Mrs. Simmons, the rabbit lady, said Diane wasn't there and I needn't come back for her. I backed out of her driveway, hit the gas too hard, and took out nearly a hundred feet of her fencing. I was oblivious to what I'd done and drove happily away.

I looked up another old girlfriend, the rock thrower, and off we went to Parkdale to visit the man who had been my neighbor with the strawberries. He was shocked to see me driving a new car. We visited for a while then left.

The gas gauge had slowly sunk toward empty and I had no money. So, we looked up my mother's third husband, Paul, the wine bottle thrower. I borrowed a couple of dollars from him, took my girlfriend home, bought gas, and was on my way.

It was late when I reached Havre. As I drove down the hill into town, Ron came flying out of a gas station I was passing and beckoned me to pull over. I did, and he got in angrily wanting to know where I'd been. I told him I'd been riding horses on a farm. I don't think he bought that, but he took me back to the motel and dropped me off.

The next day he confronted me about the crushed front fender on his car. I claimed innocence and said someone must have hit it while it was parked. Well, that story lasted for another day.

Mrs. Simmons got a hold of Ron, told him what happened, and threatened him if I ever tried to come after Diane again. When he confronted me about it, I shrugged my shoulders and walked away. I really didn't give a shit. Served him right, letting a thirteen -year-old use his car.

On Thanksgiving he wanted to take me to Bozeman to meet his parents. I didn't have a winter coat. My mother had one, but she wouldn't let me use it for the weekend because she wasn't invited to go too. So I went with just jeans and a flannel shirt. That's all I had.

His parents lived on a cattle ranch outside Bozeman. They didn't seem shocked to see him with a young girl. The whole family must have been a little odd. Maybe child molestation wasn't frowned on as much back then as it is today.

I nearly froze my butt off over there, but I made it through and didn't catch pneumonia in the process. God only knows why. When we got back from Bozeman my mother had moved us again, into an upstairs apartment in downtown Havre, with a communal bathroom.

I got a job working as a car hop nights at the local drive-in, serving hamburgers and milkshakes. I lied about my age so they'd give me a job. This was my main source of food. Many times, I would come home from working until two in the morning and couldn't wake my mother up to get in. I'd sleep in the bathtub that night, and catch my mother in the morning before she locked the door. She was self-centered and didn't give a shit.

Do I sound angry?

I had met Ron through another girl I was running with and he must have decided I was a lot more interesting kid. Most of the time he spent with me, he spent trying to get into my panties. He had a lot of scratches on his hands from me fighting him off. It seemed like most of the guys I interacted with were like that, and they were all much older than I was. I guess I seemed vulnerable because I was so much a street kid, or maybe they thought I was easy because I was young and lonely.

My school career, by now, was very sparse. I'd shot myself in the foot by telling everybody I was fifteen. I'd done this so I could work at the drive-in. However, it made me look like I was a fifteen-year-old seventh grader and I'd failed a couple of years. Now, I didn't belong with all those twelve- and thirteen-year-olds, anyway. I was too "different".

Also, my wardrobe consisted of a flannel shirt, a pair of jeans, socks, and a pair of shoes Ron had bought me. I just didn't feel like I fit into the school population. I couldn't relate to the well-taken-care-of kids.

My mother tried to force me to go to school. I think the authorities were on her back about me, or it really wouldn't have mattered to her that much. It had never mattered to her anywhere else, if I was in school.

One morning she actually dragged me to school by my shirt collar. I went, even though I could have easily overpowered her and ran. I wasn't into aggression with her. As soon as she left the school, I did too.

Ron tried driving me to school. The same thing happened there. I would wait until he drove away, then I'd take off the opposite direction and hang out on the streets.

He had it in his head that when I turned fourteen he was going to marry me. That's probably why he wanted to keep me out of trouble.

My mother condoned this plan. I wasn't excited about it, but I didn't say I wouldn't go through with it either. After all, he'd bought me my first new pair of shoes and a nice watch. I thought he was God.

One afternoon, my mother came home from wherever she was working at the time, and I was lying on the bed sleeping. She got angry about something and came raging at

me with a broom, aiming to beat the hell out of me with it. I grabbed the broom out of her hand and she fell on the bed, covering her head, and begging me not to hit her.

I was surprised by her reaction. I was in the kitchen, putting the broom away. I never did figure out what this attack was about. She probably lost it because I was supposed to be in school. I've often wondered if the authorities didn't threaten to do something legally to her if she didn't get me moving in the right direction.

Chapter 9

It wasn't long after that that I wound up sitting in a judge's chambers, with my mother, the sheriff, and a guy named Mr. Jones, the Havre school district's truant officer. Being the punk kid I was, I wanted to show these people I really didn't care what they did with me. I guess I probably didn't really care.

I was sitting in a straight-back chair and trying to tip it onto the wall, thumbs jammed into my pockets, trying to look cool. The only thing missing was the cigarette. The trouble was, there was a radiator behind me and it was hot. This was December in Montana. Every time I tipped the chair back the radiator would burn me and I would slam the chair back onto the floor. The judge kindly asked me if I'd like to move the chair. I could see the humor in his eyes.

I said, trying to be very cool and undaunted, "Naw, I'm all right." Then I continued to burn myself on the radiator. The judge smiled to himself and said nothing more about it, leaving me to my coolness.

These stupid adults were talking about me. Mr. Jones, the kindly, overweight truant officer, was talking about how I hadn't been going to school. He also told the judge about the runaways Sherry and I had done and the rodeo riders at the motel. I was really surprised he knew about that. Had he been following us around?

He brought up my sleeping in the bathtub at my mother's apartment building and he talked about her inability to take care of me, or control me. He talked about my working at the drive-in. My mother sat quiet, but agitated. Then the truant officer brought up Ron.

They wanted to know if Ron had been having sex with me. I denied knowing a Ron.   They knew I was lying, but they couldn't do anything about it. They didn't scare me and I didn't have a lot of respect for them.   What could they do to me that hadn't already been done?

Mr. Jones was making a case for the judge to order me sent to the Girl's Vocational School, in Helena, Montana, the state reform school for girls. He was doing a good job.   He told the judge, "Helen is a smart girl, but she needs guidance and someone who can take care of her. Her mother here doesn't have the capacity to control a young teen-ager.   She has already proven that, and this girl needs some guidance and some schooling."

My mother started to say something and got a dark look from the judge. Then, the judge nodded in agreement, and, with bent head, signed the papers that ordered me to be interned in the jail for the night and taken to the school the next day.

My mother said nothing until the Sheriff led me across the walkway to the jail. She ran alongside him, kicking at him and screaming. I asked her to stop, but she ignored me. Finally, the sheriff stopped, and looked at her.

He said, in a very firm voice, "Lady, if you don't stop it I'm going to throw you in a cell next to your daughter."

Well, that stopped her cold. She turned and left. I thought the whole thing was pretty funny. It confirmed my belief that adults were pretty stupid. I have to admit, it embarrassed me some and I felt ashamed of her. Why she was so upset is beyond me. She was finally getting rid of me and could get on with her life. However, she could no longer try to pawn me off to some guy so he'd take care of her.

I spent the night in the Havre jail cell singing and yelling just for the hell of it, and clanging on the bars with a tin cup. No one said a word or tried to stop me. They fed me a delicious dinner and let me rage and raise hell.

I'm sure I'd have been writing on the walls if I'd have had something to write with. I was oblivious to what was going on or what they planned to do with me. Frankly, I really didn't care. I did, however, enjoy the meal they provided. It was my first square meal in a long time. As usual, I just took things as they came, and didn't question anything.

Now, here I was, in the back seat of this kind old couple's sedan, driving slowly up a long drive to the main building of the reform school. I was being taken out of a life of neglect, fending for myself, and putting up with men messing with me. I had no idea what a normal life was, let alone what regular meals might be like. My mother provided nothing for me and didn't really see any reason why she should. I didn't even have a winter coat and it was late December of 1954.

Mr. Jones and I went into the Administration Building, followed by his sweet little wife. The administration building was an impressive, sprawling, brick two-story number.

It sported six or seven wide cement stairs, flanked by brick side-rails leading up to a porch that was half the width of the building. We entered through double glass doors. When we went in, to the right of us, near the entrance, was a doorway that led into what looked like a large living room\. There was a fireplace, that was the focal point of the homey main floor. A large mirror hung above the mantle and reflected the whole area.

There was a soft green sofa along one wall, with a coffee table in front of it. Two matching wing-backed chairs sat opposite the sofa. A desk and chair sat by a doorway that led to a hallway with two bedrooms and a bathroom. To the left of the living room was an open doorway leading to a formal dining room and a small kitchenette. This area was called "the apartment".

On the left side of the entryway was a small white-haired woman sitting behind a window in an office area. I later found out her name was Nellie McKnight. She was tiny, with a wonderful quick smile and she was old, probably in her mid-fifties. There was a closed office door in the back of the room where she sat. That was the Administrator's office.

In front of us was a stairway leading to the second floor. On the left side of the stairs was a hallway leading to some classrooms, a beauty culture room, and a large room filled with kitchen equipment. To the right of the stairs were stairs leading to the basement, where the laundry room and the garage were located.

We stopped at the front office and Mr. Jones asked Nellie if he could speak to Miss Miller. Nellie led us into the comfortable living room. We sat on the sofa, and waited.

The wait wasn't long. Within minutes, a tall, very aristocratic woman breezed through the doorway, shook Mr. and Mrs. Jones' hand, and sat down in one of the green wing-backed chairs facing the sofa. She crossed her shapely ankles and looked at us.

I can't say I wasn't a bit awed by this woman, but I still managed to hold onto my devil-may-care attitude as I listened to them planning my world and my life.

Ruby Miller was in her late 60's. She was nearly six feet tall in her two-inch pumps. She wore wire-rimmed glasses. Her hair was styled short, with a pale blue tint. She wore a soft green wool suit, with a white, long-sleeved silk blouse, that tied at her slender throat.

On her large hands were huge dinner rings. One was a large Mexican turquoise stone imbedded into a silver setting. The other one was a large black onyx stone. She waved her long, graceful hands around a lot, to emphasize her words.

I tried to act like I didn't really care one way or the other, but I took in everything. Ruby looked at me with deep, intensely blue eyes and smiled a thin-lipped smile. I glared back at her. I thought she was the most beautiful woman I'd ever seen. I decided she was going to be the enemy here. She so filled the room with her commanding personality, I knew I would have a fight on my hands to keep my tough persona. I waited to see what was going to happen next.

It may sound like I was a nasty teen. I wasn't, really. I was on the defensive, the only way I knew how to protect myself. And I would go up against and fight anyone who threatened me in any way. It's how I learned to survive.

I don't remember much about the conversation the adults were having. Miss Miller called a girl that was passing the doorway and asked her to take me to the cottage. Mr. Jones said goodbye, and I followed Gail blindly, not giving much thought to where we were going. As we walked the short distance, I looked at the huge brick building, and happened to glance up at the third floor. I thought I caught a glimpse of an old woman looking down at us.

"Who is that up there?" I asked pointing to the window. Gail looked up. She looked at me with a quizzical look in her eye and asked, whose who. Nobody's up there. That's the attic. Nobody's been up there for years." She shook her head and probably figured I was just another nut case coming into the school.

My guts churned and I felt a creepy sensation coming over me. "Are you sure? I asked. "I know I saw somebody at the window."

"No way, honey," Gail said. "You imagined it."

The door was unlocked by a tiny woman called a matron, and my life in Canady Hall began. Gail wondered off and I'm sure she was feeling grateful that she was leaving soon to go to college.

Chapter 10

Canady Hall was maybe a hundred and fifty feet from the Administration building. It was a big brick structure, as all the buildings were. There were two floors, plus a basement and an attic. As the matron unlocked the big double doors to let Gail and me in, I found myself feeling curious for the first time since all this reform school stuff started.

I didn't relate to this place as a prison. I had no idea what a prison was, so the term would have been meaningless. I'd never been in a building like this one, so, trying not to show my curiosity, I noticed everything as we moved through the building.

The little matron gave me the grand tour. To the right of the front door was a small room that housed an old upright piano. It was called "the piano room". I felt an unusual stirring, looking at that old piano. I wondered who owned it.

The next doorway led to a long living room, with windows all across the front, giving filtered light to the room because of the shrubbery outside, and the heavy screens on the windows. There were several overstuffed easy chairs scattered along the walls, and two large sofas.

Wooden end tables dotted the spaces around the sofas and chairs, with magazines on them. The carpeting was indoor/outdoor, and green. A television sat in one corner, and there was a fireplace on the wall next to it.

Several girls were lounging on the chairs and sofas. They looked up as we walked by, but weren't really all that curious, and soon went back to what they were doing. A radio was playing country-western music somewhere in the room.

Next to the living room was the dining room. Several round wooden tables, surrounded by high-backed wooden chairs, were placed around the room. White table cloths were draped over the tables because it was nearly lunch time. In the middle of the tables were set the normal condiments - salt, pepper, sugar, etc. A separate, glassed-in, dining room held a big square table, situated at the end of the room. This was the matrons' dining room. They could watch their wards from there, and we could watch the caged animals as we ate. Two girls were moving deliberately around the dining room, readying it for lunch.

We continued on our tour. The matron led me down stairs that led to the basement. She showed me where the bathroom and the showers were. I didn't know the woman's name because she had failed to introduce herself.

She was very small, like my mother, with short dark hair, on the heavy side, and, in my mind, old as dirt. She was probably in her mid-fifties. Her face seemed frozen in a perpetual frown, causing a lot of forehead wrinkles, and I had an urge to punch her. Even her voice was nasal, and angry. She was into the power she had over the girls, and she seemed to love it.

I immediately decided this was another enemy, and pretty much dismissed her as unimportant. I learned later that this matron was called "Gutsa" by the girls. That meant "little woman" in Native American tongue.

The basement was split by a cement wall into two long rooms. On the left side was a double row of sinks that ran down the middle of the room. About seven or eight toilet stalls were situated along the wall, and next to them were maybe four shower stalls. The floor was bare cement, the lighting good, and the sinks clean. However, I would not have eaten out of them!

On the other side of the cement wall was what was laughingly called "the recreation room". Problem was there was nothing to recreate with. Just a big long empty room, with some benches along one wall, a table with some chairs around it, and a door at the far end of the room. Bare light bulbs in the ceiling gave it a too-bright light. Four or five windows were set just below the ceiling, giving some light in the daytime. For the most part, it was dim and gloomy because of the shrubs against the basement windows filtering the sunlight.

Behind the door at the far end of the room was a dungeon that had been in use years ago, but had never been used by this administrator. The room was maybe eight by eight, and had a small, bare light bulb.. It had a tiny, escape-proof window near the ceiling. I didn't get this knowledge during the tour. It came later.

Back on the main floor, Mrs. Mackey, the little matron who was giving me the grand tour, took me into the matrons' sitting room, a small room across from the piano room. It was a very comfortable room, with cushy sofas and big soft chairs. She handed me a pile of clothing, bedding, and hygiene products, then she led me upstairs.

Upstairs where we slept, there were three hallways, with small, doorless rooms like soldiers, standing at attention. Mrs. Mackey led me down the shorter of the two branch halls, to a two-person room at the end of the hallway. She introduced me to Eileen. I was to be her roommate.

I wasn't used to being around other kids my age, especially not rooming with them, and, for the first time, I started feeling a little shy and nervous. I didn't show it, though. I stayed "tough" and "unaffected".

Eileen was about fifteen or sixteen. She was about the same height as me, had shoulder-length light brown hair, blue eyes, and a very solid body. She had perfect teeth and skin, and she was a beautiful girl. What she was doing here was a mystery to me. None of us ever really talked about why we'd been sent to the school. I'm not sure a lot of us knew why.

I put my things on the little single bed and began sorting through them. Mrs. Mackey left, saying lunch would be in a few minutes. Eileen didn't show a lot of curiosity about me. She showed me where to put stuff, and left to go downstairs, leaving me to go through my haul.

It included two dresses, one a gray striped thing, the other a yellow wrap-around dress that tied in the back, and had a white collar. There were socks, and penny-loafers, panties, and bras. There were sheets, pillow cases, a blanket and a bed spread. There was tooth paste, soap, a tooth brush, hair care stuff.

And, to top it off, a warm navy pea coat. My god, I thought I'd died and gone to heaven! I hadn't owned this much stuff since my mother left Joe, the farm hand. I couldn't believe my luck. There was even gloves and a warm scarf. I was rich!

The intercom announced dinner. I was still playing with "my stuff". I put it away and headed downstairs. At the head of the stairs, I noticed a door that lead to the attic. Being curious, I turned the knob, but it was locked. I put my ear to the door, thinking I heard footsteps, but, seeing Gutsa on the landing watching me, I hurried down the stairs and forgot about the door.

Another pleasant surprise was waiting for me. There was a line of girls waiting to get into the dining room. When we were allowed in, I was shown to my table by the matron. Nobody really introduced themselves, so I just kind of learned names as I went along. I wasn't the most social girl and I didn't really have any skills, so I didn't feel slighted at all. I'm not sure I really cared who these other girls were. I just followed the crowd.

The food was served in big bowls and was steaming hot. I'll never forget that first meal. The head matron, Mrs. Flannigan, liked to cook, so on Thursdays she would make her wonderful boiled dinner. It was a pot roast that had been boiled until it literally fell apart it was so tender, boiled potatoes and carrots, and a salad. I don't know what spices she used, but the food tasted like it had been cooked for a monarch. At least that's what it tasted like to me.

I had never eaten food like that before. I knew hamburgers, hot dogs, or peanut butter sandwiches, maybe macaroni and cheese, and hamburgers and milk shakes from the drive-in. That was my diet.

I ate so much that day, it's a wonder I didn't get sick from it. I absolutely gorged myself. Then came dessert. They gave us cherry pie, fresh baked by Mrs. Flannigan. I decided I was going to like this place.

The Vocational School for Girls had been opened around 1918, maybe even earlier than that. Several influential women in Montana had been raising havoc because wayward boys and girls were being housed together at the reform school in Miles City, Montana. The women didn't like the frequent pregnancies that kept cropping up there, and felt the girls should be by themselves. Whether the girls agreed or not, I have no idea. It probably took some of the fun out of life.

The school started out as a log house in Helena Valley, north of Helena, where the school was eventually built. There were six wayward girls put there to begin with.

The new buildings began to be built in 1919. The "cottages" were set up to hold fifty girls each. There were three of them.

There was a big earthquake, I'm not sure when, and one of the cottages was damaged, and condemned. They were no longer allowed to let girls live there. So, they moved some of the administration staff in there that lived on the grounds.

In 1960, Miss Miller was refusing to take more girls, and raising hell about the lack of ability to train the girls for any kind of worthwhile work. She had up to 90 girls per cottage by then and probably getting more frustrated by the minute. I can't imagine where she was keeping them!

These were teenage girls that nobody wanted. Very few of them had done anything worse than hang out with the boys, run away, and be mouthy. There was zero tolerance for being a confused teen back in those days

Every girl had to have a chore. Mine was helping with the dishes. This was sort of a start-at-the-bottom-and-work-your-way-up kind of a place, and the bottom was cleaning bathrooms, and dishes.

I had never been given a "chore" before, and saw it as a job. I knew what jobs were about, because I'd been working since I was about ten. In Seattle, when I wasn't picking fruit, I was collecting bottles and selling them. I discovered one of the bars kept crates of empty bottles behind the building. I would go back there, gather a bunch of them up, and take them around to the front and sell them back to the owner of the bar. I don't think he ever caught on. I didn't relate to this as stealing. It was just a way to get money out of an adult.

I even sold the Seattle PI on a street corner in Seattle for a while. One day, while standing on the street corner, next to a tavern, I was hollering at people to "get your Seattle PI", when a huge blimp floated by overhead. Thinking it was a space ship, I ran in to tell the bar patrons we were being invaded, and gave them all a good laugh. The job ended when I didn't give the money to the paper like I was supposed to. But then, I regress.

I took this dishwashing job very seriously. However, I'd never had a job that ate my hands off. The soap they used was very abrasive, and who knows what it was made of. But, within a week, my hands were red, raw, and peeling. I lost a whole layer of skin, and the chore was no longer fun. However, everybody had to experience the peeling hands before they could move on to something better.

Chapter 11

I was placed in seventh grade, in the little school on the second floor of the Administration building. It was early January, 1954, and I was just getting ready to turn fourteen. I had skipped so much school through the years that I was two years behind where I should have been. I probably should have been put in 5th grade, but that's not how the education dept. saw it, so, there I was, being taught responsibility and fighting it all the way. Nobody was going to tell this feisty, angry little street kid what to do!

The classroom was about the size of a normal classroom in a normal school. The teacher taught seventh and eighth grade, to a not-so-normal group of girls. She was the perfect teacher for that situation. There were at least thirty of us in class, all in different phases of elementary school. It was like going to a little country school.

Mrs. Haroldson was a woman probably in her mid-forties. She wore her long, soft, leather-brown hair in a large bun rolled up around the crown of her head. She looked like, and was, a strong, hard-working farm woman, who happened to have a degree in teaching. She stayed at the school during the week, probably in the condemned building, and went home to her family on the weekends. She was heavy, but not fat, corseted, and took no guff from anyone. She was also a very good teacher.

I didn't like school any better there than I had on the outside. I still couldn't hear well, and always seemed to be sitting at the back of the room. There were no choices in that school, and no place to run. I had to go, like it or not.

There wasn't a lot of homework, so I didn't fight too hard. None of the teachers gave a lot of homework, as it would have been an exercise in futility.

What do you do to someone in reform school that won't do their homework? Put them in the dungeon, no TV? You can't starve them. They didn't do bread and water there, so the teachers didn't have a lot of recourse. The just did what they could to get us educated.

I had one run-in with Mrs. Haroldson, and it was totally my fault. It was the only run-in I ever had with any of the staff there. Actually, that's not true. There were two others I'll talk about later.

Anyhow, this was the first one. She wanted me to sit down and shut up. I, however, felt I had the right to finish the conversation I was having with one of the girls, and wasn't going to give this old bitch even an inch. She had different ideas.

She walked to the back of the room and tried to drag me to my desk by the arm. This lady was twice my size and strong as an ox. I really had to bury the heels to even give her a little resistance.

I managed to break free of her by the time we got to my desk. Now, I was angry, and she was going to be my target. There was no way I was going to put up with being man-handled like that.

I ran at her, and pushed her. She didn't budge, and I was stunned. She took me by the shoulders and pushed back. Like a couple of Saturday night wrestlers, we, hands on one another's shoulders, pushed each other back and forth up and down the row of desks.

I called her a "bitch". She said nothing and just held on. She probably weighed 175 pounds and I maybe 100, but I was strong, and angry at everything and everybody and this was my chance to take it out on someone.

I heard one of the girls yell, "Kick her".

Then, they were all yelling for me to kick her. Before going there, I probably would have, I don't know. But, this woman had done nothing to me and I had enough sense about me to know that I didn't want to hurt her. Besides, I think I also had enough sense about me to know that this big strong farm woman could beat the hell out of me if she was pushed into it.

So, I let go, and she let go. I sat down at my desk, and she went back to the front of the room, and we moved on as if nothing had just happened. In my mind, I had won. I felt cocky and dominant, covering up my being embarrassed about acting so stupid. The girls looked at me like I was the biggest coward walking. I really didn't care what they thought. They weren't relevant to me. Nobody was.

Oddly, nothing came of the incident. I'm sure Mrs. Haroldson had to have told Miss Miller about the pushing match. I was never confronted, and graduated out of the eighth grade in June of that year with no further incidents. They took me from seventh to ninth grade in less than six months. That's the only way to do school!

One of my fondest memories of Mrs. Haroldson was her telling a story about her kids. One night, she was driving home from the school and she hit a ring-necked pheasant on the road near her farm. She stopped and picked the bird up, took it home, and cooked it the next day for dinner. Her children were freaked out that she would be arrested for poaching. She thought that was pretty funny, and so did we.

I was so oblivious to people that, when I graduated from Mrs. Haroldson's classroom, I don't remember ever seeing her again. I'm sure I did, but she didn't exist for me any more. I was used to leaving things and people behind, and never looking back. She was a wonderful woman, and it's too bad I never got to know her better. I'll bet she had a lot of great stories that are lost forever.

Ron came to see me once shortly after I got to the school. He brought my mother along, and I think he told Miss Miller he was my brother. She knew better but let them see me anyway, us sitting on the couch in her living room, with her hovering around us.

We talked about nothing. He told me how they had gone to a

lawyer to try and spring me, and the lawyer had said I was better off in the school. And, if he waited I would probably make a great wife when I got out because of all the domestic stuff they taught the girls. So, I assumed he was going to wait for me, and we would fall happily into one another's arms, get married, and become the "Beaver Cleaver" family.

Miss Miller, having left for a phone call, came back into the room, and our conversation stopped. She glared at Ron, ignored my mother then turned to walk over to the fireplace for something. I stuck my tongue out at her, forgetting there was a mirror over the fireplace.

Of course, she saw me. Ron tried to stop me from making faces at her, but not soon enough. She never said a word, or gave any indication she had seen me. I'd love to know what went through her mind.

Anyhow, my visitors left and I didn't see Ron again until I was 20 years old. He married a seventeen-year-old, took his four-year-old daughter back, and made her life hell for the next five or six years. He was a child molester, after all.

The way I found out he'd gotten married was Mrs. Flannigan, the head matron at Canady Hall. She took great pleasure in showing me the wedding announcement in the Bozeman paper. I was devastated. She thought it was funny.

I was standing on the porch of the Administration building, crying my eyes out, when Miss Miller came out and put her arm around me. She asked me what was wrong, and I told her.

She said, "You know, you should be still playing with dolls, not running around with men that age, and thinking about marriage. Why would you want to marry that guy, anyway? You'd just end up with a bunch of snot-nosed kids and a miserable life. You deserve better than that." It was an odd thing for her to say, because she really loved kids.

She gave me a big one armed hug, gazed out over the school grounds, and told me I should go back to the cottage. Then, she turned and went back inside. Somehow, she had made it all better and the hurt was gone. Maybe that's when I started to love her.

My mother came out once more that year. Not to visit, but because she wanted something. It was maybe two months after she and Ron had been there. She had moved to Helena by then. She wanted to borrow the watch Ron had given me for Christmas. She needed money and wanted to pawn it, promising she would get it out in a month. Of course, that was the last I saw of the watch.

Chapter 12

Music became my big thing at the school. There was this wonderful little woman, as broad as she was tall, that headed up the music department. She played the piano like a pro, bouncing her little body up and down to the beat of the music as she played. Even her name was musical. Mrs. Giulio. She would play "Autumn Leaves" and you could see the colored leaves falling from the trees and hear water shimmering over a small waterfall. I wanted to learn to play the piano like that.

I joined the chorus and automatically fell into singing alto. I had only been at the school a couple of months when I gravitated to the music. It didn't take long before Mrs. Giulio was giving me piano lessons.

I was beside myself with excitement about learning to play. I always loved the piano, and I was a natural. I got pretty good on it, and I think, had I started learning at an earlier age, I might have really been good.

I practiced for hours every day. I'd bury myself in the piano room at the cottage and play the rickety old thing, which was out of tune. They tried to tune it, but it just wouldn't hold and a couple of the keys were dead and unfixable. I didn't care. I loved it.

One day, we came back from school. I walked into the piano room, and there was a beautiful, ornately carved, upright piano, with all the keys working, and totally in tune. I was stunned. I had no idea who to thank, so I didn't. I just played and played on that piano.

Of course, Miss Miller had put it there. I think she was as excited as I was about my playing. It probably wasn't put there just for me, but I was the only one in the cottage at that time that played.

Mrs. Giulio was one of the happiest married women I've ever

known. She and her husband had been together their whole lives. They'd been neighbors in Boulder, Montana and they grew up together. They went to school and then on to college together. They even played "Romeo and Juliet" in the college production, and seemed born to be together. They were the epitome of what you'd imagine "soul mates" would be.

She said to me once, "Even now, after all these years, when daddy comes walking up the drive, I feel my heart jump with excitement at seeing him." And, I'm sure he loved her as much as she loved him.

They had one daughter, whom they both adored. They had a special bed built for her that rocked like a cradle when you moved in it. I got a chance to sleep in it once. and it was like sleeping on a cloud.

Mrs. Giulio had a specially built piano her father ordered for her when she was a little girl. The pedals had been raised so her short legs could reach them. She was, and still is, one of the cutest, kindest people I've ever known. Being in her presence was like walking in crisp sunrise early in the morning.

Along with the piano, I discovered, in behind the stage in the auditorium, a case holding a flute. I started playing around with it and soon was playing well enough to join the little school band. The band teacher, Mr. Porter, was thrilled to have a flute player, and he gave me lessons to help me get even better at it.

Mr. Porter was as different from Mrs. Giulio as a Golden Retriever is different from a hyena. He was dark, around the same age, sullen, sad, and full of self-pity. He had a sick wife and not much of a life outside his music. He played all the instruments except the piano, and I was determined to learn how to play them all, just for the fun of it.

He was very willing to teach me whatever I wanted to learn. The wind instruments were my forte and the accordion worked out okay, too. I never did get the hang of the stringed instruments, but that didn't stop me from trying. So I found my niche in the music department. It was the first time I'd ever had a niche to fit into.

I meandered through the first couple of months in the school, aimlessly doing what I was told, and not giving a lot of thought to much of anything. I'd been raised not to feel, so there was dead air space and total rage, but nothing much in between. I settled into the school, like a stray dog settles into an adoptive home, trying to stay out of the way and go with the flow. I didn't know how to make friends, so I didn't have any.

My roommate pretty much tolerated me, but did her own thing. She really didn't seem to have anyone that she hung out with there either. We didn't talk much to each other, and we both found that comfortable.

Sometime in March of 1955, two girls, sisters, were brought into the school. Harriet and Joan seemed too different to be sisters, but they were. Harriet was a beautiful, olive- skinned girl. She was about sixteen or seventeen. She had black, rather wiry hair that hung to her shoulders. She was tall, 5'6", or more, and very slender. She was a very sultry and French-looking girl. And, she was, oddly, well dressed. Miss Miller sent her to Canady Hall and her sister to Maria Dean.

Joan was six months pregnant. She was shorter than Harriet by a couple of inches, had short dark hair and a more muscular, stocky build. She laughed easily, unlike her darker, "Adams Family" sister. Harriet was mysterious and fascinating. Joan was fun, and funny.

Harriet seemed worldly and very intelligent, which meant she could be a trouble-maker. They had come from California, and that alone made them celebrities. Eileen and Harriet became friends, and I was included, even though I was quite a bit younger, emotionally and age-wise.

Miss Miller didn't like Harriet much. I think she could smell trouble brewing and had concerns about the girl getting me and Eileen, "the good girl", into trouble. And she was right. It didn't take very long.

Eileen was a tomboy at heart. She had been raised on a farm with seven boys. She was strong and tough. She exercised daily, which consisted of jumping over the hedges in front of Canady Hall in the summer, when we went out to sun ourselves. At night, before lights out, she would get totally naked. I kid you not, totally, and she'd walk up and down the halls while doing the back bend.

Nobody, not even the matrons, thought this was odd. A naked girl in a backbend going past your doorway and down the hall was just Eileen doing her exercising. Soon, it was no big deal to me either and I stopped even noticing her.

My roommate was not just pretty and well-built. She was also very talented. She would design a pattern for a dress, blouse, you name it. And before you knew it, it was a fashion. She made all her own clothes and was allowed to keep and wear them. All the girls could wear their own clothes as long as they weren't slacks, or jeans. I'm sure Eileen had other talents, but the sewing was incredible. I was very impressed.

Easter was coming. Harriet and Eileen decided the four of us, including me and Joan, needed new Easter outfits. Eileen created the patterns for them, now all we needed was the material.

I worked in the laundry on Saturdays, and they came up with the idea that, if I could get my hands on a couple of sheets, they would make really nice outfits. The following Saturday I worked on the mangle. That was a fun job.

Lots of scary stories flew around about the dangers of the mangle. We talked while we worked about girls getting their hair caught and not being able to get loose before the thing turned them into a pancake. It was scary but fun stuff and we relished scaring hell out of any new girl working on the machine.

I managed to take two bed sheets out of the laundry and back to the cottage. Nobody questioned why I was carrying the sheets when I left the Administration building, or when the matron let me into the cottage. They just took it for granted somebody had told me to do it.

One of the other girls managed to confiscate some pink and blue dye, and we were on a roll. Eileen and Harriet worked on the outfits for a couple of weeks. They sat in our room and sewed all four of them by hand.

The skirts were the regular basic banded skirt you learn to make first in sewing class. The tops were high-collared, short-waisted, works of art. When they finished them, somehow they got the cook to let them into the kitchen, and they were able to dye and starch them.

The outfits were beautiful. Joan's was a maternity outfit, dyed pink. Mine was blue. Someone had donated some hats to the school for the girls for Easter. I picked mine out, a small white hat that fit over the crown of my head. It had blue and pink cloth flowers on it.

We wore them proudly to the Easter services in the auditorium on Easter morning. We even had nylons to wear. All four of us sat together and felt like royalty in our new clothing.

Nobody said a word about our new clothes when we left the cottage. I'm not sure anyone noticed what the outfits were made out of. However, Miss Miller paid attention to everything. Just before the services started, she walked up to my chair, bent over and whispered in my ear, "Nice outfits. We were wondering what happened to the missing sheets." She walked away with a little smile on her face.

I know I must have flushed. Eileen heard her too, and just stared straight ahead. We were busted.

I have to give her credit. Ruby didn't usher us out of the Auditorium and make us strip. However, the outfits mysteriously disappeared that night and were never seen again. I don't know if Eileen and Harriet got into trouble over it or not. I sure missed mine though. It looked great with the new Easter hat!

Chapter 13

I discovered God around that same time. I hadn't had much religious exposure before I got to the school. My mother told me I had been baptized Methodist as a baby and I went through the praying for the toy dog to become real, but lost interest when my prayers weren't answered. However, praying worked for the Easter hat.

When we lived in Fort Benton with Joe the farm hand, there was a Lutheran minister that lived across the street. I would visit his wife and small children once in a while. I was curious about the "God" thing, and asked her a lot of questions.

One day I asked the minister's wife where God came from. She looked at me in some confusion then she said, "It's not right to ask a question like that. You have to have faith that He's always been here."

"But, how did He get here? Where did He come from?" I innocently pushed.

"It's a sin to ask questions like that. You must have faith," was her frantic answer.

I never went back to see her again. All that faith stuff just didn't make any sense to me. However, in the school we said the Lord's Prayer and the Hail Mary every night before we went upstairs to bed. I decided God would be the father I never had, and I called him that.

When I first saw the Easter hat, I found myself praying that I would get to have that hat. When I got it, I decided it wasn't right to pray for something that you were in competition for. It was an unfair advantage that you were taking. So, I never prayed for anything again that was competitive. Nobody was teaching me this stuff, so I had to make it up as I went along.

My first runaway occurred in May of that first year. Several of the girls, including Harriet and Joan, Harriet being the instigator, decided to make a break for it. It was springtime and the natives were growing restless. I had no particular reason for running. I just wanted to be a part of something and wasn't able to discriminate between right and wrong. I had no place to run to, but I went along just for the hell of it.

A group of judges from around Montana were having a get-together at the school to talk about who knows what. The chorus and the orchestra was supposed to perform for them. The shindig was to take place in the gym.

So, about five of us planned to go into the gym, and exit out the side door, when nobody was paying attention. Miss Miller would be busy hosting the judges, and girls involved in the music were trusted to behave and do the right thing.

Harriet was the ringleader, and I have no idea what her motive was. I and the others just went along for the adventure of it. I was to stick with Joan, who was now very, very pregnant. Harriet would stay with the other two.

So in through the main door and out through the side door we went. Eileen was not in this group. She didn't do music, and she was getting out the following year. She had no intentions of screwing that up any more than she already had with the Easter outfit debacle. So off we five girls went.

There were no high prison fences around the school. There was a barbed-wire fence to keep the livestock that belonged to some farmer in, but nothing to keep us in.

Joan and I slowly lumbered to, and through, the barbed wire. Harriet and her group were long gone across the field. Joan and I were walking like we had just gone out for a little stroll in the pasture. It was obvious we were not going to get very far, but we weren't thinking that way. We were just playing "follow the leader".

A small herd of horses came up to watch the two bipeds plodding across the muddy spring pasture. Their curiosity gave me an idea. I said to Joan, "Hey, why don't we catch one of those horses and we can ride it to the highway?" Of course, I had no idea the highway was several miles away and probably lots of fences in between. Also, I never gave any thought as to weather the horses were broke to ride. It was just a matter of, do what seemed obvious, with no forethought; typical teen-age thinking.

Joan, being as naïve as I was, agreed. She gave me her head

scarf and I walked up to one of the gentle creatures, a big bay. I wrapped the scarf around his neck. He stood as still as any steed you'd want to ride. Joan was supposed to give me a leg up, after which I would somehow manage to pull her up onto this guy's back.

We were doing fine. Joan cupped her hands together and I stepped into them. I pushed up with my leg and threw my other leg over the back of the horse. Just as I was about to let myself down on his back and expertly guide the big animal to our escape, one of the other horses shied. I landed on thin air as my mount raced out from under me to join his herd, galloping across the pasture as if they were being chased by wolves.

I remember thinking this was going to hurt as I landed butt first on the mushy ground. I was no worse for wear, but very embarrassed when I got up. And, to add insult to injury, the horse took off with Joan's scarf. She was laughing so hard, she literally rolled on the ground, holding her big stomach. I, however, didn't think it was all that funny.

When I got up and pulled Joan to her feet we heard a car horn honk. Looking around, we saw the blue Ford station wagon that belonged to the school coming across the pasture. Driving it was Arlette Livingston. She was the assistant superintendent of the school.

Arelette was big, maybe two hundred pounds, and was about 5'5" tall. She had gleaming, dark brown hair that hung past her waist. The girls loved to brush it when she let it down. She wore it in a braid curled around the back of her head most the time. Her voice was a deep contralto, and it rang out like the liberty bell when she laughed.

This woman was a mixture of caring, kind gentleness, extreme intelligence, and a raw nasty violence that came out if you crossed her. I'm pretty sure she was a lesbian, when lesbians were not supposed to exist. She didn't seem angry, but she could turn black if you doubted her power. She also had some strong ideas about how the school should be run, and they didn't coincide with Miss Miller's.

The school had a starch paddle that normally would have been used to stir vats of starch. But in this case, it was used to paddle girls if they got out of hand. When Miss Miller used it, which was rare, she'd give three or four good swats on the butt and called it good.

When Arlette used it, it was, "Bend over and grab your ankles." Then, she'd hit the girl until the victim cried out. It was a big deal to try to stay silent as long as you could when you were getting it from Arlette.

The paddle was about the thickness of a one-by-four, made out of hard wood, about three inches wide, and a tapered foot in length. It had a hole in the wide receiving end. I was lucky it was never used on me, but I understand it stung like crazy. It was a brave girl that could take the lickin' and not complain. We would gather outside the room while the paddling went on and count the swats.   The more swats she took without yelling, the more respect she received from the other girls.

Harriet got paddled once by Miss Livingston, I don't remember why. She never made a sound. That really pissed the batterer off and Harriet got the hell beat out of her, stubborn girl.

Anyway, Miss Livingston stopped the car and called us over. Joan and I meekly walked over and got in. I think we were both relieved. It was cold out there and there was no point to running from her, anyway. As we sat in the back, she wanted to know where the other girls were. We told her, truthfully, we didn't know. They had gone way ahead of us and we were just trying to make it easy for Joan.

"Horse didn't work out for you, huh?" Miss Livingston threw her head back and gave a big guffawing laugh. "Too bad. It might have been fun chasing you two across the field on that horse."

Neither one of us thought that was very funny, but she laughed all the way back to the school. We must have gotten nearly a city block away.

Miss Livingston took us to Canady Hall and left us with Gutsa. She took us to the basement and had us sit on the benches in the "recreation" room. We found a box of Kotex in the bathroom and entertained ourselves by tearing it up and throwing it around the room. It's amazing how much material is involved in one Kotex pad. The room looked like a fluffy snowstorm had hit it.

We sat there giggling and tossing cotton from the Kotex, when Miss Miller walked in, flanked by several of the judges. She was giving them a tour of the cottage and wanted to show them just how neat and clean the girls were.

It was too late to turn the judges back as they shoved their way into the basement room. She tried to distract them from the snowfall going on in the rec room, but I'm sure they noticed. She looked at us with a wilting look that only she could produce and quickly managed to turn her entourage around and headed them back up the stairs.

Joan and I looked at each other and got the giggles. We'd really outdone the phrase, "getting into trouble". The punishment for that fiasco was no movies for two weeks and
clean up the recreation room.

Joan was moved back to Maria Dean and soon left to have her baby. I never saw her after that. They brought Harriet back, having found her in Texas. She didn't stay long. I don't know why. She may have turned 18 soon after she came back.

Chapter 14

Lil Bit was a little Native American girl, who was in the school when I got there. There seemed to be a disproportionate number of Native girls in that school. I don't remember what Lil Bit's real name was. I think it might have been Theresa. Everybody just called her Lil Bit.

She was maybe four feet, six inches tall and probably weighed less than a hundred pounds. She had short, dark permed hair that stood out around her head like an afro. She was seventeen at the time, and I don't know how long she'd been at the school. Everybody liked and respected her. She was feisty and smart-alecky, cute, and fun to be around. She also had a very good head on her shoulders and got good grades in school.

Lil Bit's best friend was Mary O'Leary. Mary was about five

feet, nine inches tall, and a big muscular girl. She was strong as an ox and gentle as a newborn lamb. She also was Native American. She was pretty, with long, shiny black hair that hung past her shoulders, a beautiful smile that exhibited perfect white teeth, and a wonderful sense of humor. She was about fifteen or sixteen at the time.

Lil Bit and Mary were inseparable. They reminded you of Mutt and Jeff, and nobody messed with either one of them. They went everywhere together.

One evening, after supper, I went down to the basement to wash up and get ready to go upstairs to bed. I'd only been in the school for a few months. Scuttlebutt had it that something unusual was going on in the basement and I was curious too.

As I came through the doorway, I saw several girls gathered around Mary and Lil Bit in the recreation room. I ambled in to see what was going on.

Lil Bit and Mary were having a fight. The tiny girl was screaming at the giant, "I'm going to beat the shit out of you, bitch!"

Mary was dancing around her angry little friend, laughing, her beautiful face in crack-up mode, fists in the air, inviting a punch. "Go ahead, you little shit. C'mon, see if you can catch me!"

Lil Bit moved in for the punch. Mary stretched her arm out and placed a huge hand on the little girl's forehead. Her hand covered Lil Bit's head like she was holding a baby. Lil Bit began throwing punches that landed on nothing but air. She was getting madder by the minute, as she threw punch after punch to no avail. She twisted and turned and couldn't get her head out of Mary's giant paw.

Mary was laughing so hard she could hardly hang onto Lil Bit's struggling head. She finally couldn't maintain the hold any more and stop her spasmodic laughing. Suddenly, she let go, sending Lil Bit flying past her, and barely catching herself on the wall before she ran headlong into it. When her enraged little friend turned back around, there was Mary, on the floor, holding her stomach from the pain of squealing with laughter.

Lil Bit put her hands on her hips, Gutsa style, and said something like, "That'll teach you to mess with me, bitch." She stalked out of the room and up the stairs, her head held high, looking victorious. Tears ran down Mary's face, as her hysterics continued. The audience just stood around in wonder.

The next day, the two were back together like nothing had happened. That's the way it was in the school during the first couple of years I was there. Nobody held grudges, or wanted to kill anyone. It was just a bunch of unwanted girls that nobody knew what to do with, except for Ruby Miller. She had concerns about each one of these wonderful girls, and showed it often.

For every funny situation that happened in that school, there seemed to have to be a tragic one, as well. Many, if not most, of the girls had come from backgrounds where they weren't taught social skills, or proper ways to behave. They knew survival skills and many of them were very tough. Many times they took things into their own hands when it didn't seem like the powers that be were going to handle things soon enough.

Case in point: A young, thirteen- or fourteen-year-old girl, dirty blonde hair and acne tearing up her pretty face, shy - a nondescript person - came into the school. Her name was Sally, and, looking back, she sort of reminded me of me.

She was placed in Canady Hall and got the room right next to Eileen and me. Sally kept to herself, and tried to go unnoticed, but, unfortunately, she had absolutely no decent hygiene habits. She never seemed to bathe, and she got to smelling pretty strong.

Many of the girls were complaining about her, and nobody wanted to sit next to her in the living room, dining room, or at school. She never talked to anyone and seemed sad and scared all the time.

One of the girls ransacked Sally's room one day and found a bunch of used Kotex in her closet. She reported it to the matrons, but nothing was done. Finally one morning, I was down in the basement washing up before breakfast when I heard voices and crying, coming from one of the showers. I went to look and see what was going on.

There were no doors on the showers. Four girls had Sally naked in the shower and they were scrubbing her down with a very course scrub brush and lye soap. She was crying from pain, but also, I think, from the humiliation.

They finally let her go. She covered herself with a towel, and ran upstairs. I don't think she missed a daily shower after that. And there were no more complaints about her body odor.

Also, it turned out that the reason she kept the used Kotex in the closet was, she would wash them out and reuse them. I can't imagine what the environment was like that she came from before she landed in the school. Hell, even I knew better than to reuse Kotex.

I know the matron on duty that morning, Mrs. Flannigan, knew what was going on in that basement. I think she just decided to let the girls mete out their own hygiene education in their own way. Maybe she thought Sally would learn it better coming from the girls. Or, maybe she just sadistically enjoyed the whole idea of what was happening to the unfortunate kid.

It was a cruel thing for a matron to allow to happen. I doubt if anyone told Miss Miller about it. She would have thrown a fit. In my later years there, I would have tried to stop it, but I was too young and too new to step in and maybe get the hell beaten out of me.

Soon, Sally was gone too. Maybe sent to Maria Dean, maybe somewhere else. All I remember is, she wasn't there long and then she was gone.

That winter of 1955 we got a new matron, Miss Martin. She was young compared to the other matrons working at the school. She was probably mid-forties and very inexperienced. The girls liked her because she seemed to like them, wasn't power hungry, and gave us all some slack. Also, I think we kind of related to her as one of us. She was a bit immature, and not very in control. She was probably not a good mix for a reform school employee. She had been recently paroled from prison and was being given a second chance. We wanted to help.

One night, several of the girls decided we should have a séance. We'd been sitting around in a circle in the basement, talking about ghosts, when the idea came up. We decided we wanted to talk to a ghost and Mary O'Leary said she knew how to do it.

So, we set up a table with chairs around it, turned off the lights, and eight or ten of us positioned ourselves around the table and held hands. The rest of the girls stood and watched.

There was a soft ghostly light making its way into the room from the washroom area, and a light glow coming through the small windows from the full moon. It was an eerie evening and the excitement was high.

Mary spoke in a soft voice, calling for a spirit to show itself. Everything was quiet. Nothing happened. Her voice became more droning and commanding, and she insisted on some sort of sign. Someone said the curtain in the window fluttered. The goose bumps were starting to chill as we sat there quietly waiting for something more to happen. The tension grew. Mary droned on, calling for any spirit to give a sign.

The small curtain on the basement windows seemed to drift again. Someone screamed and sent the girls that were watching stampeding for the stairs. We at the table held our ground. Mary called some more.

Suddenly, there was movement. The hands holding mine went rigid. Then we felt the heavy table begin to rise up off the floor. That was it. We couldn't maintain any calm at that point. Everybody at the table jumped up together, screaming blood-curdling screams, and headed for the door, tripping and falling over each other. A couple of them were crying.

A few of the girls actually made it to the stairs. Some of us landed on the floor and lay there cringing when the lights flipped on. We looked fearfully at the table, and there, crouched under the big table, was Eileen, laughing so hard tears were rolling down her face. I think she peed her pants from laughing so hard. The whole incident left us all very shaken. Oddly, no one got mad at her for pulling a stunt like that.

The girls that didn't see "the ghost" were totally freaked out. Miss Martin was freaked out and there was no way she was going to settle the girls down. She called us all for prayers and, instead of the usual prayer, she prayed for protection and safety from evil spirits we might have conjured up, which freaked us out all the more.

After prayers, we went up to bed, but none of us got much sleep. Of course, it didn't help that a couple of girls took it upon themselves to hide under beds and grab ankles of girls trying to get ready for bed! The screams were blood-curdling. The screams of laughter that followed sent chills up the spine of a fourteen-year-old girl who had never really spent much time with people.

I never did really learn to adjust to it all. I just took it as it came, as usual. Most of the joking around, I never really got. I guess

I took it all as picking on, because my mother's jokes had been so mean-spirited.

The poor matron, Miss Martin, spent the night fielding bad nightmares, and had a run-in with the night matron over the whole affair. She was let go shortly after that. Probably because, emotionally, she was too much like the girls she was trying to oversee.

There was another ghost incident while I was in the school. I was maybe sixteen at the time. It was summer and several of the girls went home for the three months. The ones left in Canady Hall were moved to Maria Dean so they could give Canady a good cleaning and a new paint job.

One night, some of the girls who were over there helping, came home freaked out. It seems Mrs. Flannigan had taken them up to the attic for some reason and there were bare-footed footprints going up the dusty stairs. The scary part was there were no footprints coming down the stairs, and no other way out of the attic. Even Mrs. Flannigan saw them, and they were never explained.

There was a dungeon cell made of hard wood up there. It had

all sorts of names drawn in crayon on the wall. Dates from 1940's and drawings of people in red crayon adorned even the ceiling. Someone got mighty bored in that cell.

The scary stories ran hot and heavy in the school. I think teens lend themselves nicely to horror stories, especially judging from all the horror movies involving teens that are put out in this day and age.

There was a story told about when the school had gardens and grew their own food. They had a root cellar somewhere on the grounds where a lot of the vegetables were kept. The story went that there was a girl in the school who had epilepsy. She took a powder, but, instead of running across the fields, she went and hid in the root cellar. It was winter, and she had a seizure down there, passed out, and froze to death. She wasn't found until spring.

True or not? Who knows? It was a good story and added to the belief that her ghost haunted the place. It was a great story for a spooky Saturday night down in the basement.

Eileen and I had a falling out after the ghostly basement fiasco. She decided I guess, she didn't like me any more, or was afraid I'd get her into trouble and screw up her release, I don't know. Maybe she scared herself a bit that she would do something crazy like that.

Also, she had gotten her hair cut in the Beauty Culture class and I got all silly and upset about it, like teens will do. But, I don't think that was it. Kids are changeable, especially teen "juvies" like us. Hormones and all, I guess. Anyway, what she did to get rid of me was, she started popping chewing gum at night, which for me, was like raking fingernails across a black board. It drove me to distraction, and she kept it up until I asked to be moved.

They moved me into the room next door where Sally had been, and again, I had my own room for the second time in my life. It was probably eight by ten and doorless. There was room for a single bed, a dresser, a small rocking chair, and a closet. A heavily screened window gave me a view of the driveway and the valley to look out over, and I was fine with it.

Again, I never looked back. Had no feelings one way or the other about it all, and just moved on. Eileen was released to go home around Christmas that year. I saw her once more when she and her husband came to visit Ruby, maybe a year or two later. She never even acknowledged me, even though I walked through the living room where they were visiting. I felt just a twinge of sadness, then it was gone, and Eileen became the past and was forgotten.

Chapter 15

I don't know if I discovered religion/God, or religion/God discovered me. It was fall, 1955, and I was emotionally lost, as usual. I guess I was in need of something to cling to. I didn't really have any friends at the school, and I had no idea how to do friendship. I kept mostly to myself. Anybody I made friends with had to be intelligent, assertive, interesting, and reaching out there for me. I never reached out for anyone. I really didn't know how.

The friends I did make kept disappearing as they got into trouble. I didn't have the skills to create lasting friendships. I don't think most of the girls there did either, nor did

they want lasting friendships coming out of a reform school. I honestly didn't relate to this place as a prison for teen-age girls. It was just a place where I lived. On the "outside" people looked on the place as a prison for teen girls. Sort of a dumping ground for the lost and unwanted.

Anyhow, there were church services every Sunday morning and you could go if you wanted to. It was something to do, so most of us went. A different preacher from a different denomination came out every week. The favorite for the girls was an Assembly of God minister. He was maybe mid-forties, dark hair that fell into his face when he got going, and an olive complexion that gave him a rather dark demeanor.

He had big, expressive, brown rolling eyes that would bug out of his head when he made a point. He ranted about the coming of Christ and what would happen if you didn't obey his laws and accept him as your savior. He'd say something frighteningly awful about what the devil was going to do to us if we didn't shape up then stand looking at us with his eyes bugging out. Sometimes, to make a point, he'd jump at you. The effect was so silly at times we'd burst into laughter. Other times, it would scare hell out of us.

The minister acted like he didn't notice us laughing at him. He'd pause for effect and then move on like nothing was going on. He'd stomp and pace back and forth in front of the auditorium, ranting as he went. Sometimes, his death threats were so intense we girls would go home and have nightmares about the devil that night.

Ruby would sit in the back of the room with a glower on her face and look like she was wishing the guy into his own hell. She was a Christian Scientist and she totally disapproved of the raucous way this minister put out his message. I don't think it was just the lack of dignity concerning the whole thing. I think she also didn't like the way he scared the girls. Sometimes, she'd just get up and leave in disgust.

The guy sure got our attention, though. Some of the things he told us would happen if we weren't pious were pretty scary. The fear never lasted long and we went back to being teen-agers within a day or two. That minister was sure memorable, though.

Somewhere in this mishmash of religious teaching, I decided God would be my family. I never really had a father so I related to God as my father and talked to him like a daughter. I'd never had a significant relationship with a man that wasn't hell-bent to getting into my panties, except for Joe the farm hand. But the way he treated my mother was so bad, it made me a little afraid of and angry at men. I also decided, somewhere in my subconscious, that nobody would ever treat me like that, and they never have. There've been threats, but the look on my face always prevailed.

I didn't have any real fear of this God that the ministers went on about. He seemed pretty safe and caring, the way I saw him. I wanted to find out everything I could about him, so I read through the Bible three or four times during the years I was in the school.

The stories were fascinating and I was beginning to feel like this God was my buddy. I carried the Bible everywhere I went, like a security blanket. I had very little, if any, self-talk back then, so had no way to determine how I came off to other people, or what the girls in the school might think of me. I was oblivious to everything but my own inner life, and imaginings. In all honesty, I guess I really didn't care all that much what anyone thought. I'm not sure I even realized it might matter some day.

Needless to say, my behavior didn't make me popular with the other inmates. I was graduated into ninth grade that fall. I took my trusty Bible and went off to classes. My first or second day in ninth grade, I was sitting in English class and the teacher had been called away.

The kids, as kids will do, got a little rowdy. Karen, my old runaway buddy from Havre was in the class. I didn't even know she was in the school. She lived in Maria Dean and I hadn't seen her up until this point. I don't know how long she'd been there.

Some of the girls decided I was going to be the one picked on that day. They were teasing me about carrying the Bible around, which was confusing. I didn't get what the problem was. It was a book. Big deal!

They started throwing balled-up paper at me. I just sat there and ignored them. A pencil flew past my head. Even Karen was throwing things and making snide comments to me. Then the teacher came into the room and everything stopped.

When class was over Karen passed me looking very ashamed of herself. She never said a word to me. But, in a place like that, the best way to get into trouble with the other girls was to not go along with whatever they were doing. That was the only time I remember seeing her at the school. She must have gone home shortly after that. There were no good-byes.

My feelings weren't so much hurt, as I was embarrassed and wondered why they were doing what they were doing. I didn't feel scared, didn't have enough sense to be scared. If anything, I think my lack of any reaction scared the other girls because they pretty much left me alone after that incident.

What people don't understand can be really frightening, especially if they can't get some kind of a reaction going and they can't gain control.

The minister that really got my attention, though, was the Youth for Christ minister, Dan. He would come to the cottage on Saturday nights with his plain, gentle, long-suffering wife in tow, and tell us about his program and the kind of work the missionaries did. He was young, maybe early thirties, very good-looking, and energetic. His wife would sit there looking lovingly at her husband, like he was wearing a halo.

Dave told us about some missionaries that had gone into the jungle in South America to try and convert some native people that were reported to be headhunters. They landed their plane, tried to meet with the natives, and were promptly killed, and beheaded. I'm not even sure they got a chance to say hello.

Dave said the government, presumably the American government, gave the missionaries ten years to rehabilitate those people, or they were going to go in and obliterate them. There was oil, or minerals, they wanted in that jungle. Never mind the land belonged to these under-rehabilitated headhunters and, who knows if this story was even true. But, at fifteen I had found my calling and my goal was set. I would become a missionary and help save those poor people from obliteration. That goal, like most teen goals, lasted nearly six months.

Chapter 16

It was because of Dave, the Youth for Christ minister, that I pulled my second runaway. Don't misunderstand, it wasn't his fault. I just badly needed someone to talk to, and he came to mind. It never dawned on me that I could ask Ruby to take me to see him. I just decided to go. I didn't connect running away from the school as a criminal act. I never really "ran away from". I just never related to myself as being "locked up".

Helena was about seven to ten miles from the school. When you're that age you don't look that far ahead. You just "take it as it comes". So, off I went. I don't even remember how I got off alone. Maybe I left the laundry one Saturday morning. I walked across the horse pasture, stopped to watch a couple of baby skunks playing outside their hole-in-the-ground den, and went on.

It took me several hours, a torn dress that got caught on a barbed wire, and a very dirty girl in need of a bath, but I made it to town. I walked into the Youth for Christ second-hand store looking like I'd just come out of a fight with a cougar. An old woman walked up to me, looking nearly as disheveled as I was, and asked what I wanted.

I told her I wanted to talk to Dan, and could she call him for me. I told her where I was from and she freaked. She told me to get out of the store and don't come back. I was stunned. This was supposed to be a godly woman working for a representative of Christ, and she was uncermoniously kicking me out of her store, for fear she'd get into trouble. I started to cry.

I had no money and I was exhausted from the walk to town. She finally had enough mercy on me to let me use her phone after I begged and pleaded with her. She, however, made it plain she wanted me to tell them that it wasn't her fault I landed in her store. I called the school, and Arlette answered the phone.

"Well, it's about time you called. We've been waiting all day," she said. "Where are you, and who is that mumbling in the background?" I told her where I was and that the woman was really upset.

Arlette said. "What on earth are you doing there? You don't belong there, and I want you out of there now. Meet me in front of the Parrot restaurant."

I obeyed, and walked the two blocks to the Parrot restaurant. She came and picked me up. Nothing much was ever said about the incident. Needless to say, we saw no more of Dan. I later realized I had probably dodged a bullet by not being able to find him. I found out he liked to play around on his wife and who knows how he might have taken me running away to talk to him. He had seven kids, so he liked his sex.

You'd think the people at the school would have realized that I was having a rough time. Nowadays they would have gotten me somebody to talk to, to find out what was going on. Back then, it was just chalked up to teen-age confusion I guess. So I went on my lonely way back to the piano.

It was during this period of time that Ruby told me she wanted me to write an essay on "Why I Loved America". The Helena school system was having a contest and she wanted to enter me in it. Where she got the idea I could write is beyond me. I know at some point she was interacting with my grandmother in Blackfoot, Idaho. Maybe she told Ruby something about my writing prowess as a little girl.

When I was a little girl, second and third grade, I used to write little stories about animals and their adventures. I'm guessing this is where Ruby got the idea I could write.

I had no concept of "America". I barely had the concept of states, and even then, the idea of them didn't ring any bells for me. So, I did what I seem to do best, even today. I winged it.

I don't remember a thing about that essay. I'm sure it was mostly double talk and rambling. I don't even know if she actually entered the thing into the contest, or even if they allowed it to be entered, because of what the school was.

When I asked her about it a few weeks later, she off-handedly said, "Oh, you won second place."

I didn't give the thing another thought. I didn't even ask what I'd won. I'm not even sure I knew there were prizes in a thing like that. That was one of the weirder experiences I had with that wonderful, mysterious woman.

Chapter 17

Life went on at good old GVS. I practiced on the flute and the piano ad nauseum, until I was sounding pretty decent. Mr. Porter asked me if I would like to play in the Helena Symphony Orchestra. I told him I didn't think I was good enough for that, but he insisted, so I became second flute in the orchestra. Mr. Porter played first flute.

Miss Miller took me out and bought me a long black skirt, a long-sleeved black top with a plunging neckline and silver jewelry, with black heels to go with it. The orchestra had a rule about showing bare arms. Nothing about plunging necklines was said. I looked very classy in that outfit, and felt very sophisticated.

The wonderful conductor looked exactly like what you would expect a conductor to look. I don't remember his name any more, but I'll never forget the way he looked.

He had long flowing gray hair that fell into his face when he sent the orchestra into loud crescendos with his baton flying through the air, and his great head keeping a sharp jerking time to the music. Beethoven must have looked a lot like that when he conducted his music.

We'd go over and over a measure until it was perfect, then he'd take us over it another ten times. He could send you melting into his praise, or cringing under a look of disgust when you hit the wrong note. He expressed to the orchestra once what a beautiful tone I pulled out of my flute as I played an especially moving solo and I nearly fell apart with pride.

I was the youngest person in the orchestra and I still think Miss Miller may have pulled a couple of strings to get me in. I didn't have the technique it took to play some of that music, but I sure loved trying, and the sitting in the middle of all those wonderful musicians. I never really felt a part of it, but the music was incredible and I kept up most of the time.

One of my fondest memories of playing in the orchestra was a young girl that was brought in to play a concerto on the piano. She was thirteen and had been playing since she was two years old. Her father was a surgeon and very well off. He had brought in a teacher from New York, whose sole purpose was to teach this girl how to play the piano.

She practiced with us once and came back to do the concert. I was shocked that she had memorized the whole piece. I don't remember what she played, but it was complicated and she played it like she'd been practicing it for years.

Before the concert I ran into her backstage. I asked her if she was nervous. She looked at me with a blank look and asked, "About what?"

I just shrugged and went out to sit down on the stage. She played beautifully and didn't make one mistake. I guess she wound up living back east and making records. I always thought she'd get really famous, but I guess not. Her sister, however, wound up singing for the Metropolitan Opera. Wow, and I knew them when!

Our conductor was an instructor at the University of Montana, Missoula, and was the head of the music department. He played a mean violin.

One of the concerts headlined him playing Beethoven's Concerto for violin. I'd never heard anything more exciting and beautiful. I had no idea a violin could be made to sound like that. Playing two strings, harmony and melody at the same time seemed impossible to me, but he was doing it. I can still hear it when I think about it, and it brings tears to my eyes.

Then, of course, there were the screw ups that sent the

conductor into fits of temper and wanting to throw his baton at someone. And it wasn't always one of the orchestra members.

There was a guy who was a pianist who played a concerto with us. We practiced together some, and when the night of the concert came along, we all felt pretty confident about it. Everything was going swimmingly, when, suddenly the music tilted and we were in symphony hell. Nothing sounded right and the conductor kept looking at the pianist, who continued to obliviously careen along through the music. There was rustling in the audience as people realized the sound was off.

What happened was, the performer had skipped a whole page of the music and was playing way ahead of the orchestra. We had no way to catch up so we just kept playing. He finally realized the sound was off. He looked up at the conductor and managed to get back on track somehow. He wasn't invited back to play again! I of course, thought the whole thing was pretty funny. Still do.

There was the oboe player who fouled up a solo part that dancers on the stage were supposed to be dancing ballet to. They finally stopped and just looked down into the pit at her and the orchestra bravely moved on.

Then they added a young girl who had been playing the oboe for maybe six weeks. She played like she'd been playing for years. Her brother was also in the orchestra and played the clarinet. He got a little crush on me and would come visit once in a while at the school. Miss Miller was thrilled that he showed an interest in me.

I, however, wasn't particularly attracted to him. I just loved his playing and his talk of music. His hair was wiry and wild and he was kind of weird, like most geniuses are. He went on to the State University in Bozeman and became a professional student. He would write me long letters telling me about his music. He was into Jazz and called the clarinet a licorice stick. He was nerdy, but fun.

I played in the symphony for two years, and quit when they got a new conductor. I was seventeen. The whole thing changed and wasn't fun any more. The experience sure gave me a love for classical music that I enjoy even today.

Sarah came into the school when I was just turning fifteen. She was a fascinating girl, maybe sixteen, and she was brilliant. She would read encyclopedias for fun. She'd go through the dictionary every day, pick out a new word, and use it all day long.

Sarah was obviously raised in an upper-middle-class home, and I have no idea why she was placed in that school. It might have had something to do with her nymphomania, I don't know.

She was a pretty girl except for her front teeth being a little too big, which messed up her smile a little. She was about five feet seven inches tall and had an enviable hourglass figure.

Back then a figure like that was considered really sexy. She was blonde-haired and blue-eyed, and had skin that carried a perpetual soft golden tan.

She played the piano like she'd taken lessons for years, and probably had. She also played the bass fiddle. She had a wonderful contralto singing voice and sang alto along with me in Mrs. Giulio's chorus.

She played in the Helena Symphony with me, but she wasn't as impressed with it as I was. It did give her a chance to get close to some of the guys in the orchestra. Whether she took advantage of that or not, I don't know.

She thought it was very stupid that you couldn't bare your

arms during a concert.

Miss Miller had also bought her a beautiful long- sleeved, black sweater blouse and ankle-length skirt to wear. I thought the outfits were cool. Sarah thought they covered too much.

Her comment about it was, "Wow, it sure doesn't take much to turn the audience on if bare arms will do it. Makes you wonder who's in the audience!"

Sarah and I became friends, as friends went in that situation. She would come home from the Administration building and regale me with her escapades while she was over there. She'd sneak out of class and go down to the garage. She'd catch one of the maintenance men that worked at the school and play with him, getting him chasing her around the cars, and eventually he'd catch her and they'd have hot sex in the back of
the school's station wagon.

She seemed to feel she needed to conquer all men, and she did a pretty decent job of it. She'd get Mr. Porter behind the stage curtain in the auditorium. They'd have sex and she'd whisper enduring love words to him. Sadly, he believed what she said was true.   He was totally in love with her.

Miss Miller knew nothing of Sarah's antics. I think she had a lot of denial about people like Sarah and she didn't realize that she'd hired a couple of real scumbags to work at the school.

Sarah went home for a few weeks visit one summer. Mr. Porter told me he had gone to the town where she was from and tried to see her. She was totally stunned that he would show up there and she told him to get lost.

He was crushed by her rejection. He should have known better. He was old enough to be her father, or maybe even her grandfather. Talk about denial. Shortly after that, he was giving me a clarinet lesson and he told me about his visit and how she'd hurt his feelings. I'm not sure why he thought it was safe to tell me. This was a guy who was married to a very sick wife and had grown children. He even cried while he told me about Sarah. I sure felt sorry for him.

If I'd have told Miss Miller half of what I knew about some of the people that worked in that school, half the staff would have been fired. Of course, she would not have believed me. It was incredible, some of the people that were drawn to a reform school full of wayward girls. It wasn't Miss Miller's fault. It's just the way it was in those days.

I doubt if much has changed in the prison systems since then. They are always going to attract some controlling people who are willing to take advantage of vulnerable inmates.

Sarah came back from her summer vacation and it soon became apparent that she was very pregnant. She thought the whole thing was pretty funny because the baby's father was the local Catholic priest in her town. Hell, I didn't even know she was Catholic.

The priest actually had the nerve to come to the school asking to take Sarah back to his parish so they could take care of her until she had her baby. I don't know how he got wind of it. She probably wrote to him bragging about it.

Needless to say, Miss Miller was having none of it. She threw a fit and told him, in not a kind way, to leave immediately, or she'd have him thrown out. I think she would have beheaded him if she could have gotten away with it. I seldom saw her get that angry. I don't know how she knew what was up, but I know she knew. And she didn't put the blame on Sarah.

I look back on this now, and it angers me that no help was gotten for Sarah. She obviously had a serious problem and needed counseling, not a bunch of adult males taking advantage of her. I often wonder what happened to her.

All the girls came to the aid of Sarah while she was pregnant. They always became very supportive of any girl that was pregnant out there. Sarah enjoyed the attention. Then, one night she was whisked away to the hospital in labor. She came home a few days later with her figure back and the baby gone.

Sarah had signed the adoption papers and didn't even know what sex the baby was. She really didn't care and just wasn't interested. After she healed up, she went back to her sexual appetites, including Mr. Porter. Eventually she got involved with one of the other girls, and they stayed involved until she went home when she was 18 and graduated. I guess she got bored playing with old men.

Chapter 18

Sarah was a fun friend and we had some great times. We took Latin together just because we thought it would be fun. Miss Miller, at our request, had the gym teacher teach us Latin. Sarah caught on fast. I never caught on at all. I think my poor hearing made learning new languages difficult for me.

She and the teacher would read something out of the Latin book and laugh. I'd sit there confused, and they'd explain what it said. Usually, it was something stupid about a bear.

Miss Miller tried so hard to make the school a worthwhile place for kids to learn something. I read an article in the local Helena paper after I got out of the school, saying that the cooking classes and the beauty culture classes and even the baseball team started after the man took over when Miss Miller died. That's just not true. All of those classes, and the baseball team were going on when I entered the school in 1953. Miss Miller was responsible for starting those classes.

Back to Sarah: You could get into wonderful conversations with this intelligent young girl. She knew a little bit about everything. She laughed and joked around a lot, and spent a lot of time talking about male conquests. She played the piano so well I'm amazed she wasn't asked to perform with the symphony. I was never jealous of her playing, but tried to emulate it. I learned to play a lot of the things she played, just not as well. I could boom out "La Traviata" nearly as well, driving Miss Miller, who was downstairs in the main building, crazy with the noise.

Sarah had a brilliant mind, and when tested, was found to be sophomore college level knowledge when she was a sophomore in high school.

Today I'm sure Sarah had gone through some serious molesting when she was small. None of us girls really talked much about our backgrounds, so I don't know much about her before she came to GVS. Back then I just thought she was exciting, daring, fun, and a little shocking.

Her female partner was a girl called Alisha. When she first

came in, Alisha had pyorrhea. She wasn't allowed to use any of the dishes or utensils that the other girls used. There was a fear of her spreading the disease. You would see her after meals washing her dishes in the janitor's closet and putting them on a shelf there. I felt so sorry for her being singled out like that, even though it was necessary. It probably bothered me more than it bothered her.

Eventually, she was taken to the dentist and had all her teeth pulled. She was fitted with a complete set of false teeth and she was only 15.

Alisha was slender, and boyishly built, not real pretty, but smart, in her way. I really felt bad for her that she had to get false teeth. My mother had false teeth and I knew how much trouble they were for her.

After Alisha had been at the school for a few months, Miss Miller decided she was going to take her to Butte and have an evaluation done by a psychologist. Why, I never did find out, nor did I ask. I didn't even think to ask. So, when Alisha told me about going, it sounded interesting and fun. So, I decided I wanted to go too. I was fascinated with people and how their minds worked, and had read everything I could get my hands on in the school about psychology. I was curious about people who worked on people's heads, and Miss Miller agreed to let me go.

So, off to Butte, Montana the three of us went to visit the psychologist. I went in first. The guy was a short, heavy-set, balding man, with thick, wire-rimmed glasses, and a boring attitude. He was using the Rorschach test, and I had a great time with him. The test is also known as "the ink blot test" which is what it is. The trick is to tell the doc what forms you can see in the ink spots.

I'll bet I found at least ten or fifteen different forms in every card he held up. If I didn't see it I made it up and made him believe I was seeing it. He would look at the card and say, "Where are you seeing that?"

I would run my finger around the card, and say, "See, there's the head, the eye, etc."

And, incredibly, he would agree that he saw it too. He'd ask, "Why have I never seen that before?"

I ran him clear past lunch with my crap and he was getting "antsy" to go eat. He finally made me stop, as I was pointing out yet another form that I was claiming to see. I walked out of there laughing my head off. I thought he was one of the stupidest people I'd ever met. He sure was gullible, or was it me? I don't know.

Miss Miller took us to lunch and then Alisha went in to spend some time with the little man. We waited for her to come out and the three of us headed home. Alisha told me that the doctor had told her to hang around me more, because I was a "very together" girl, and she could learn from me. I nearly fell of the car seat laughing about that. He sure didn't change my mind about adults.

Chapter 19

There didn't seem to be anyone that cared about these girls on the outside. Very few of them had visitors coming to see them on weekends. These were the girls that nobody wanted, so they were sent to the school to get them out of everybody's hair. However, Miss Miller really loved many of them and wanted what was best for them. Thus, the psych evaluation, if she thought it would help her understand them better. I really believe she would have done more, had the governor been willing to cough up more money.

As I said earlier, Alisha became Sarah's sex partner in time. At one point I told her I was going to interfere because I didn't think it was right for two girls to be messing around. Alisha begged me not to say anything to Sarah, because she felt I was the only one Sarah would listen to if I asked her to stop. I let it go and never said anything, deciding it wasn't that big a deal, and it was none of my business anyway.

Ruby loved dramatics and loved putting on plays. She not only directed them, but she made all the scenery for them, chose the cast for them, and sweated over all the little details. The only thing she didn't do was the music. Mr. Porter and Mrs. Giulio took care of all that. And the plays were always operettas, so there was a lot of music.

I also think Ruby wanted to show the public that these girls were not just a bunch of juvenile delinquents. They were real people with real talent and very much worth trying to save. They weren't just "throwaway" kids. She took a lot of pride in the plays she produced.

We put on three plays while I was at the school. The first one was a thing called, "The Little Troubadour". It had a love interest, a main character, and a villain. I don't remember exactly what it was about, but my part was the little barmaid love interest of the main character.

The main character was the troubadour, played by Sarah. A very strong, powerful-voiced Native American girl played the villain. Her name was Carol, and she was incredibly talented. She had this wonderful booming talking/singing voice that carried throughout the gym without a microphone. She sang a loud pure alto and she was one of the funniest people I knew.

She used to tell a story about her crazy brother. She said that her alcoholic father woke up one night to find her brother leaning over him with a butcher knife. His eyes were wide open and wild. Apparently, the brother was walking in his sleep. She said she heard her father screaming, and before she could get to him, he was out of his bed and running out of the house in terror.

Her brother never woke up. He just put the knife down and went back to bed. She never said it, but my guess is that the father was abusive and the brother didn't like him much. When she told the story she would act it out, doing both the brother and the father's parts. She was so expressive the girls would go into hysterics just watching the whole thing.

Now, it seems tragic to me that they would have to live with someone like a father that they wanted to kill, but then it was just funny to a bunch of girls who probably came from a similar background.

Carol had very little self-consciousness when she performed and she loved to goof off. Brown-skinned, with short black hair and dark brown eyes, she probably stood all of five feet three inches and seemed like she was a giant. Some of it was in the powerful voice, and some of it was her carriage and attitude.

She was physically very strong and boyishly built. She had an air about her that said, "You don't want to mess with me", and nobody did. I don't think she ever got into a fight out there.

She wasn't aggressive so much as assertive and sure of herself. I'm sure if someone would have been stupid and pushed her, they would have gotten the hell beaten out of them, but nobody did.

There was no reason to. She was very well-liked by everyone.

Carol must have been about sixteen. She was another "throwaway". I think Ruby loved this girl, too. She was proud of Carol's talents and encouraged her to use them as much as she could.

Arlette Livingstone told me once, when I was an adult, that Ruby's love was conditional. I think that's probably true. She probably did home in on the very intelligent and talented girls. Not that she ignored the others. She just paid special attention and gave extra time to the ones that stood out.

She would spend a lot of time grooming them and pushing their abilities. She wanted them to learn what they were capable of and use their gifts to have a successful life. That was her job, after all. It's what she had dedicated her whole life to.

There's a wonderful parable that could have been Ruby's motto. A little boy is walking along a beach after a powerful storm. The beach is covered with thousands of beached starfish, brought in with the high waves. The little boy is picking up starfish and throwing them back into the water.

A man is sitting on a log, looking out at the water. He's bitter and unhappy, and wondering what life is about. His life is not going well, and he's feeling very sorry for himself, wondering "what's the use?"

He calls to the little boy walking on the beach. "I don't understand why you bother to throw those starfish back in the water. There're thousands of them on this beach that will die. What difference does it make if you throw a few back?"

The little boy picked up a beautiful orange starfish and tossed it into the sea. He looked at the man and said, "It made a big difference to that one".

Through Miss Miller's years of working with kids that needed her so desperately, I'd guess she threw a lot of starfish back into the water to give them another chance at life. Before coming to the school, she had worked in the Montana school system her whole career and had taken on at least one kid that I know of, who was born very crippled.

She had been living with a couple in a rented room when the boy was born. He was very deformed and the mother quickly lost interest in caring for him. Miss Miller took over, took care of, loved, and taught the boy, until the mother got jealous and accused her of having an affair with her husband. Ruby moved out at that point.

She had raised and worked with the boy on math, which he was quick to learn. He went to college and became a Certified Public Accountant as an adult, making a great living for himself, and proving he could be a successful member of society, even in a wheelchair. He visited her once at the school and her pride in him was inspiring. He obviously loved her deeply.

She introduced him to me when he came to the school. He had to be carried up the front stairs by his driver. He told me he owed his whole life to Ruby. I felt very proud of her.

Miss Miller was a Christian Scientist. She had joined the religion because her sister was a practitioner. When I found out about her religion, I decided to look into it. One evening I was sitting in the living room reading "Science and Health with Key to the Scriptures", when Carol walked in. Carol was Catholic, as were a lot of the Native American girls.

She walked up to me and said she wanted to see the book I was reading. I marked my page and handed it to her. She thumbed through it and then suddenly, she threw it on the floor. I looked at her stunned.

She said, "If I was caught even touching that book, I would be sent straight to hell. It's sinful for a Catholic to even look at a book like that."

She was serious. I couldn't believe what she was saying. I've never heard that since, and I'm not sure the Catholic religion teaches that it's sinful to look at other religions. It
sure scared Carol, though. I think all of us girls were a little bit "drama queen". We were teen-agers and bored. Not a good combination.

We put on "The Little Troubadour" for the governor and some of the town's people. We did it in the gym and the building was full of people from Helena. The Governor was there with his wife and my guess is that most of the rest of the audience were part of his entourage. Half the Capitol was there.

Miss Miller was always trying to get more money out of the governor and I'm thinking this was one of the ways she did it. Trying to prove these girls weren't dangerous criminals. She was backstage fussing around with makeup and fixing costumes. She was more nervous than we were, but I think she was having a wonderful time. She was in her element.

While the play went on, she stood in the wings with the script, prompting the actors. Mrs. Giulio was at the piano, bouncing up and down as she played the opening music. Everybody was excited, adrenalin was pumping high, and we were ready.

The whole thing went off without a hitch. There were no serious lapses of memory, the music was great, nobody's voice cracked, and the audience thought we were wonderful. The governor and his wife came up on the stage, after the curtain calls, and had their picture taken with the cast. His wife looked nervous and kept watching the exits.

She had on this beautiful brown mink stole and I couldn't keep my hands off the soft shiny fur. I would guess the picture that was taken shows me petting the woman's stole. I had no couth when it came to protocol. I didn't know what was and was not done with these people.

Mrs. Governor was much too nervous about being surrounded

with all these reform school girls, to ask me to knock it off, even though she gave me a rather scared look. The look just prompted more petting. Miss Miller finally caught my eye and gave me "the look". I got the picture then and left the poor woman alone.

As soon as the photographer finished snapping the important people of the state, they were gone. I'll bet Mrs. Governor gave a sigh of relief as their driver closed the door of their car.

A couple of the girls that were down on the floor as ushers were standing in a corner giggling about something. They said a woman they were ushering in with her friend, said to her friend, "My goodness. These girls look as normal as any girls I've seen in town."

One of the ushers heard the comment. She sidled up to the woman and said with an evil grin, "We may look normal, but you never can tell. It's really only a show."

The woman took on a panicked look and watched her back throughout the whole play. We all got a huge kick out of that. I'm sure Miss Miller would not have seen the humor in it. She was trying so hard to pass us all off as normal.

We did such a good job with "The Little Troubadour" that we

were asked to perform it at the professional theater in town. We were all scared to death, but the play got a standing ovation. Miss Miller was thrilled, and so were we.

The only faux pas during the play was made by Carol. She was supposed to say, during the final scene where the villain is confronted, "You were tickled pink Todoro, when you found out ---- whatever."

Instead, she said, "You were pickled tink, Todoro, when you found out, etc." She brought the house down. The audience howled with delight and so did the cast. I didn't know someone that brown could flare that red, but she did. It was the only time I ever saw Carol embarrassed. However, she didn't miss a beat with the script and much to everybody's delight, she bravely kept going, and finished her accusation.

The rest of the cast pulled it together and kept up with Carol. We were nothing if not professional. The trick was to keep going and not become hysterical with laughter. Miss Miller, standing in the wings with her trusty script, blanched at Carol's mistake, and stood looking horrified. When she realized her cast was moving on without falling apart, she gathered her composure and went back to her prompting. We got wonderful reviews in the newspaper. And, as an added bonus, nobody ran away that night.

Carol, Sarah, myself, and four other girls rode home with Miss Miller in the blue Ford station wagon. The other members of the cast rode home with Arlette in the green station wagon.

Nobody knew where we were from. Unlike today, back then the state emblem was not required on the cars. Miss Miller would not allow the cars to have special markings on them to show where they came from. Most of the state-owned cars were a bright orange, which she wouldn't be caught dead driving. So we had a blue and a green Ford station wagon, both big as boats, that we got hauled around in.

Our driver, as usual, was driving very fast as we headed out of Helena city limits, out into the big flat valley where the school was located. We didn't quite make it out of the city limits when the revolving lights went on from a car behind us, and a cop pulled us over.

Miss Miller had a grim look on her face as she pulled to the side of the road, the police car pulling up behind her. Arlette brought up the rear of the little caravan and stopped behind the cop car.

The officer walked up to our driver's side window. Miss Miller rolled the window down, and looked at the young officer with a glower on her face. He had no idea who he was dealing with. We girls held our breath and waited for the explosion. This lady was not one to be messed with.

She asked him in a stern voice why he had stopped her. He told her she was driving seventy miles per hour in a fifty-five mile an hour zone. She told him flatly that he was wrong and obviously wasn't paying attention. He looked at her in astonishment, and she added, "Young man, do you know who I am?"

He said very politely, trying to sound firm and brave, "No ma'am, I don't know who you are. Now, if you'll give me your license, I will find out who you are."

She begrudgingly handed him her license and let him know she wasn't very happy, and would be having a talk with the governor in the morning about the incident. She needed to get these girls back home and it was getting late.

The officer walked back to his car as she grumbled under her breath that she wasn't speeding and who did he think he was stopping her, anyway? She sat there gripping the steering wheel and glowering out the windshield, waiting while the officer checked her license.

The girls sitting in the back of the station wagon giggled to each other. The two of us sitting in front with the sizzling woman held it down, and waited to see what would happen. I was fascinated with her attitude toward the cop. Even I would have behaved in a more respectful manner. I figured the older you were the more leeway you had with the police. I've found out as an older person, that isn't necessarily so. You have to have "the look".

The young officer came back to the car and returned Ruby's driver's license. He looked a little chagrined. He said politely, "I'm sorry to have held you up, Miss Miller. I hope you'll be more careful of your speed in the future."

Miss Miller gave the poor guy a wilting look and said, "I wasn't speeding, young man." She put the car in gear and tore away into the night.   The officer stood watching her and looking helpless.

I looked back at Carol. She looked at me with a grin, and mouthed, "She was speeding."

I nodded my head in agreement and mouthed, "I know". That was one of the incidents that gave me an indication of how wonderfully powerful and pompous this incredible woman could be. And she was able to pull it off. I'd never been around someone like this, and I was amazed and in wonderment over her.

During the three years I was at the school, we also put on "Huckleberry Finn", the musical version. I played "Puddinhead Wilson" and Carol was "Injun Joe". It was a fun little play, and, again, people were invited from town to see it. The Governor and his wife didn't make an appearance this time.

The play turned out well, but it wasn't as good as "The Little Troubador". The scenery, which had been painted by Ruby, was wonderful, even down to the Mississippi River painted in the background. I think painting that scenery gave her some peaceful time, in a more and more turbulent world that was brewing at the school.

Chapter 20

For some reason, Miss Miller was fussy when it came to me, right from the beginning. She was very insistent that I was going to be a lady. Yeah, good luck with that!. She was that way with all the girls, but, more so, it seemed, with me. For example, nobody was allowed to wear jeans or any sort of pants. This struck me funny, especially just before I started writing this book.

I managed to track down a niece and nephew of Ruby's, and they sent me pictures of her in her younger years. She was born in the late 1800's. She was born back east and landed on a homestead outside of Augusta, Montana when she was 18. In two of the pictures, she is wearing pants. One is her on horseback and the other is her horsing around on a bridge with another lady, both dressed in very bizarre attire, very unladylike!

And she was a teacher!

Anyway, when I came into the school, I was a smoker. It was a part of my persona, the cigarette hanging out the corner of my mouth and the thumbs in the belt hoops of my jeans. I thought it made me look tough. Well, no more. It was dresses and penny loafers, and no cigarettes.

The other girls that smoked were given half a cigarette five times a day. I still don't know if there was an age requirement, or she just decided I wasn't going to smoke, but I became a non-smoker while I was in the school. She seemed to have a little bit different set of rules for me than she did for some of the other girls. I know she was in touch with my grandmother during part of the time I was out there, and maybe that had something to do with it.

I hadn't heard from my grandmother in years and I have no idea how she knew I was even in the school. But I do know that she and Miss Miller planned my whole schooling future, and neither one of them was happy when I didn't go along with it. But that comes later in this story.

I began to see Miss Miller as a surrogate mother. She seemed to care a lot about me, and was very impressed with my musical talents. As I grew to love her, I was willing to do whatever she wanted me to, within reason. It was important to me that I pleased her, and, even though I didn't have a good concept of other people's feelings, or thinking, and I truly believed that all adults were stupid, I still tried to be what I thought she wanted me to be.

I took to writing her little love notes. The notes would always start with, "Dear Mom". I would tell her about my day, or say silly little things that a girl might say to her mother. They were almost diary-like. They always ended with "I love you".

This was the first time I ever told anyone I loved them. I think it was the first time I ever really loved anyone in a deep meaningful way.

I would slip the notes into Ruby's pocket, or hand them to her before I left to go back to the cottage after school. She always read them, but she never said anything about them. I don't know what she did with them. Probably threw them away. It would have been very inappropriate for her to even allow me to write them in that day and age. Back then, I guess the boundaries were still a little hazy between inmate and keeper.

Being allowed to talk to her through notes sure kept me from being so lonely and it made me feel like I belonged to someone. Probably, it helped me keep my sanity as well. There were no counselors for us to talk to. It was the first time I ever shared myself with anyone and I was totally committed to this woman.

Once, I actually called her "mom" to her face. She got all flustered and said, "Don't call me mom out loud. People will think you're my illegitimate child." I swear this is true. And she was serious. Remember, she came out of the late 1800's morality codes. I never called her "mom" out loud again. But I did continue the notes.

Miss Miller filled a huge hole in my life. As I said earlier, I had been very alone and neglected as a child. My mother never said she loved me, or showed me any love. For example, once, when I was maybe six or seven, I had been home alone while she was at work. I ate an apple, and was just finishing it when I saw her coming up the walk. I wasn't supposed to eat anything until she got home.

I got scared and tried to flush the core down the toilet. It plugged the toilet up, and when my mother came through the door, the flood was moving into the living room. I had no idea what to do.

She rushed passed me into the bathroom, crying from frustration. As she plunged the toilet to get the apple core out of it, she screamed at me, "Damn you. I wish you'd never been born!" Her actions throughout my time with her certainly reinforced that comment. It still hurts when I write it. It's a very cruel and damaging thing to say to a child.

So, when Miss Miller came along, she made me feel special, cared about, and loved, and I think I would have died for her if she'd have asked me to. I think she loved me, although sometimes she had a funny way of showing it. I adored her. I was always looking for ways to do special things for her.

Ruby had dozens of handkerchiefs. I think she had allergies and used a lot of hankies. I, when I started working in the apartment where she lived, would gather up her hankies and take them down to the laundry. I'd wash every one by hand and iron them dry. It was definitely a labor of love and she never complained about it.

One night, before I went home from doing the dishes, I went in and turned her bed down. I guess she had a visitor, some dignitary from the state that evening. She was showing him around the apartment and there was her turned-down bed. She was embarrassed, and told me not to do that again. I didn't.

Miss Miller had, probably, the first king-sized bed ever made. It was specially made for her and was longer than a normal bed and much wider than a double. She was so tall that her feet hung over the end of a regular bed. She had a pink satin bedspread on it, and it was very feminine.

She also loved hats and had several of them. But, oddly, I never saw her wear a hat. I guess she'd buy them just because she liked them. She was as soft and gentle as she was tough, no-nonsense and strong.

She had strong feelings for most of the girls that came into that school. She was a perfect person to run a place like that, although, in the end, I think it broke her heart.

Chapter 21

Miss Miller didn't look on the girls as bad. She looked on them as needing guidance and people to care about them. She was constantly frustrated that she couldn't get more money so she could do more for them and the school. She wanted a swimming pool in the worst of ways, but the governor wouldn't budge, and accused her of trying to run a girl's finishing school, and not a reformatory. She was up against a no-win, but she kept fighting. However, when she died and a man took over her job, a swimming pool was put in. Also jail cells appeared on the property. Ruby would have had a conniption fit if she'd have known.

Going through teen-age years was rough in a place like that. You had the confusion and the craziness of the teen hormones and nothing to try it all out on, unless you wanted to get yourself into trouble. So, that's what some of the girls did - got themselves into trouble. I'm sure some of them tried their hormonal rages out on each other. Some of them just ran away, some of them screamed and fought, and some just ignored the hormones, or got depressed.

I sort of used them on the piano. I spent hours playing, usually in the Auditorium in the main building. I was a loner and spent most of my time that way. I didn't have the skills to make friends like most kids. There was no giggling on the bed, talking about boys. I'd been the guy route, usually with men way too old for me, and I didn't have much in the area of sexual feelings. I saw men as users. As a matter of fact, sex really kind of disgusted me, so I didn't give it a lot of thought.

I was very mixed up, and had no idea how to fit into the general population. The girls pretty much left me alone and I didn't pay much attention to them. I spent a lot of time playing various instruments. I'd sit and play for hours, mostly classical music, and some old songs from back in the 40's.

As I got more trusted, my duties during the week were to go over to the main building and, along with another girl, wash the dishes in the little kitchenette. The cook at Canady Hall would send food over for Miss Miller, and whoever else was eating with her. Usually it was Arlette and Nellie Knight.

After they ate, we would clean up the dishes and I would go upstairs and play the piano for an hour or two, while the other girl would go back to the cottage. Ruby never questioned me about this. She just accepted it and, maybe even enjoyed it.

One evening, I was wrapped up in "Fur Elise", and Ruby came up behind me and watched me play. I had very long hair at the time. She ran her fingers through my hair, didn't say a word and just stood there. Then, she left as quietly as she had come and went back downstairs. That was the only real physical affection she ever showed me.

One evening, when I was ready to go home, she asked me why I played so loud. I was surprised by that. I didn't think I was playing loud. She sent me to have my ears checked a few days later, and I was found to be profoundly hard of hearing.

She asked me when I came back, "Well, did they find a bunch of wax in your ears?" I told her no, that they found that I was very hard of hearing. She got up and headed for a telephone and never complained about my hearing again.

I didn't know I couldn't hear, but it sure explained a lot about me and the way I acted, my shyness with people and my problems with school. When I was in first, second, and third grade, I spent a lot of time in trouble for talking too much. Well, when you can't hear, you talk, or fall asleep.

I wasn't ready for a hearing aid at that point, according to the doctor, but everybody was more understanding of the need to repeat themselves for me sometimes.

In later years the doctors determined that I'd had Rubella when I was very small and it had caused massive infections, which ate up the bones in my ears. I remember getting very sick at age three.

My mother and I were staying with a strange woman that my mother said was my godmother. The woman had several kids that were older than me. She would make a huge pot of goulash and keep it on the stove for everybody to eat. That's all everybody ate. When it was gone, she made more. It was a wonder nobody got food poisoning from it.

I don't remember a lot about that situation. I do remember when I got sick, they brought in a doctor. He had them close all the drapes in the bedroom, to keep it dark so I wouldn't go blind. When he left the room, he turned to the woman and I heard him say, "Fix this kid some eggs, for god's sake." That must have been when I had the measles, and lost my hearing.

Miss Miller had a couple of cats. A gray Manx, whose name I can't remember, and a big white cat she called Punky. The cats had no interest in anyone other than her and they were fair game for some of the girls. Every once in a while, a squall would ring out and a white tail would disappear around a corner, headed for Miss Miller's room. She would come running to see what had been done to her beloved cat. Neither cat was ever hurt, but they did get a lot of teasing from the girls.

One of the girls who worked in the apartments with me was Shelly, a pretty blonde, blue eyed girl of around 15. One night, on the way over to the main building, she told me she wanted to run. I tried to talk her out of it, but she was determined. She didn't have any particular reason. She just decided she was going on the run.

What was I supposed to do? They knew she left with me. I told her I'd give her a twenty-minute head start. Then I had to tell Miss Miller. There was nothing else I could do, and I wasn't going to lie to Miss Miller.

Shelly agreed and took off across the pasture. I went on to the main building, went upstairs, and played the piano for twenty minutes. The weird thing about this was, the matron always called the administration building to let them know we were on our way. Nobody questioned why I was upstairs playing the piano, instead of working on the dishes, and no Shelly with me.

After giving Shelly the twenty minutes, I went back downstairs in tears. I found Miss Miller sitting in her chair in the living room, and told her Shelly had taken off. Miss Miller said irritably, "Why didn't you tell me when you came in?"

I told her, crying my eyes out now, that I had promised Shelly a twenty-minute head start. She told me to stop crying and go clean the kitchen. Then she went to call someone to go get the girl back.

They brought Shelly back the next day. Some of the girls were calling me "snitch". Shelly told them I had snitched on her and nobody spoke to me for weeks, other than to make nasty comments about my "tattling". There's no logic in young, juvenile delinquent teens, I guess. I had very little choice but to tell Miss Miller what was going on. The anger didn't make much sense to me.

A few weeks before Shelly took off, Miss Miller had a birthday. Her favorite cake was angel food. Shelly and I decided to bake a birthday cake for her. The kind-hearted cook at Canady gave us permission to bake the cake, and a recipe for it. We baked a beautiful angel food cake from scratch and frosted it with pink powdered sugar frosting.

We proudly took it to the apartments with us and presented it to Miss Miller that night. She was pleased, and shared it with Arlette and Ms. Knight. They had cake and ice cream while Shelly and I did the dishes. When we left to go back to the cottage, she gave us the rest of the cake to take back and share with the other girls.

As we walked back to the cottage, we couldn't think of one good reason why we should share our masterpiece with a bunch of girls who wouldn't appreciate it, so we sat down on the grass, in the dark, and ate the rest of that cake.

There was about three quarters of it left, and both of us got a pretty good belly ache from it. I don't know if Miss Miller ever found out why the two of us got so sick, but I'm sure she and the other two women made some fairly accurate assumptions. And, again, nothing was said, no questions asked.

Chapter 22

The entertainment at The Girls Vocational School was sometimes interesting and varied. There were dances once a month. I was told that before my time people from town were invited out for the dances. There was a live band from town, and refreshments. Problem was, several of the girls got pregnant. Hmmm. So, the invites stopped and the girls danced with each other. I'm pretty sure Miss Miller paid for the bands out of her own pocket. I can't imagine the budget stretching that far.

The dances were held in the gym. Some of the girls from Maria Dean would decorate with crepe paper and balloons. The refreshment table would be set up with colorful non-alcoholic punch and cookies, and everybody would be filled with excitement. (We were easily entertained.)

I have memories of dancing with Miss Miller a few times. She never asked us girls to dance, but never turned down a girl if she was asked. She was a wonderful, smooth, ballroom dancer, but didn't get off on the "jumping up and down" we did to the faster tunes. When Elvis came into being, she actually liked him. I couldn't believe it. Even I was too snobbish back then to admit I might enjoy his music. She thought he was a wonderful young man. Go figure.

One snowy winter Montana night, we were supposed to have a dance. It was very cold and blustery and, rather than have the girls be disappointed, Miss Miller hired two bands. She sent one to each of the cottages and we danced in our living rooms. She visited both cottages and joined in the fun.

I'm not sure if she was concerned for our health, or she had some concerns that someone would try to run away in that awful weather and freeze to death in the pasture among the horses. I also have no idea where she found an extra band on such short notice, but she did.

And talking either one of the bands, let alone both, into coming out on a night like that must have been a Herculean task. She must have given them her whole month's pay check. Anyhow, the two cottages danced the night away until midnight, when the girls had their smokes and we were sent upstairs to bed with rock and roll pounding in our heads.

As I said earlier, Miss Miller wanted a swimming pool for the girls, but it was not to be. So, in the summer we were taken to a nearby lake to go swimming. Usually Arlette Livingston and other female staff would take us. Arlette would wear this funky swim suit, with a little skirt going around her huge waist. She was so big that she actually would fall asleep floating in the water on her back. The amazing thing was she was so buoyant she never sank. She wasn't self-conscious about her weight at all. She looked like a huge whale in a two-piece swim suit, floating around out there.

Arlette seemed to enjoy being with the girls and did a lot of things with us. Miss Miller did things with us too, but I think she was busier with day-to-day stuff and political things than Arlette, and that's the way they broke up the work.

Miss Miller liked to tell stories. She told us about how she and some of the other staff used to take the girls outside the fence around the place. They'd build a fire in the middle of the night, roast marshmallows, and tell tall tales. The girl who told the best one got a prize. She would laugh when she talked about some of the unlikely tales the girls told.

She talked about being in Great Falls, Montana when she was younger. She was assistant assessor for Cascade County at the time. The singer, Marion Anderson, was performing at one of the major hotels in town. Because she was black, the management wouldn't let her stay at the hotel where she was performing.

Miss Miller and several other women in town marched on the place with placards touting the unfairness of the hotel's policies, and finally, the management relented and gave Ms. Anderson a room. She was very proud of that incident. Boy, would she be proud to see what's happening today.

She told stories about her and another woman coming to Helena from Minnesota, headed for Augusta, Montana. She was 18 years old and it was the very early 1900's. They had to ride the stagecoach from Helena to Augusta, which is probably a hundred fifty miles. They teased the driver the whole way, pretending to be afraid of being attacked by Indians, who were long gone onto the reservations by then.

Miss Miller was a teacher and was going to Augusta for her first teaching job. When she got there, she made a claim and set up a homestead. She rode horseback to work and, with help, built herself a cabin. She was nothing if not very independent.

She was born in 1891. She had six brothers and sisters. Her grandfather had been a hellfire and brimstone preacher. Millersburg, Minnesota is named after him.

Apparently, he decided Armageddon was going to happen on a certain day, and true believers were supposed to meet on top of a hill near Millersburg, to be lifted off to heaven. His followers sold all of their belongings and headed for the hill. They waited, and nothing happened. So, Rev. Miller decided he'd made a mistake with his dates and they met a few weeks later on top of the hill and tried again. Nothing happened. They all went home, and tried to put their lives back together.

Miss Miller's niece told me that Rev. Miller went back to his house that day, and the door was locked. He knocked on the door and his wife called out, "Who is it"?

"It's your husband," he called back.

His wife said through the door, "You can't be my husband. He was taken to heaven this morning." Evidently, she didn't buy into his beliefs.

According to the internet, he had a following of over a million people at one time. His teachings were the basis of one of the evangelical religions that we have today. Miss Miller chuckled when she talked about him.

She also loved to tell jokes and drop little dry comments that would send you rolling in the aisles if you caught them. She'd laugh at her own jokes. She was very self- conscious of something I don't know what. She may have had false teeth. She never laughed very loud, like Arlette did. She had this tight little cross between a laugh and a chuckle, her mouth barely open. But her sharp blue eyes caught everything and sparkled with humor when she laughed.

Miss Miller always took the seniors on their "sneak day" close to graduation. The second year I was at the school, she took me along with them. That year, she took the seniors to "The Gates of the Mountains" outside Helena. There's a beautiful lake, surrounded by small mountains that goes on for miles. Somehow, she talked the Captain of the boat we were on into letting me steer the thing. When we got close to the mountains he showed me how to turn the boat in such a way that it looked like you could open and close the mountains like a gate, thus the name.

He took us several miles up the lake to a picnic area and we all got off the boat. We played and picnicked for several hours before he came back to get us. It was great fun for me and I think for the other girls. I'd never really been on a picnic before, so it was a new experience.

The seniors didn't seem to mind that I was included on their sneak day. I wondered, sometimes, why they didn't pick on me, call me Miss Miller's pet, stuff like that, but they didn't. Arlette told me later when I asked her about it, that they seemed to sense that Miss Miller really loved me and I loved her. And, I never acted special, or asked for any favors. It never would have crossed my mind to ask for anything special. I never saw myself that way.

Miss Miller took me on a few excursions during the time I was at the school. I've always thought she was trying to teach me manners and how to behave in public. Maybe she enjoyed having me with her, I don't know.

She took me out to dinner one night after a symphony concert. The restaurant was very posh. I'd never been anywhere like that, but, hey, I'd read "Emily Post" and I had manners. We had a great dinner and I didn't screw up and use the wrong fork or anything. I was a total lady and Miss Miller was proud.

When we finished she asked for the check. The waiter told her a man at the next table had paid for our dinner. He had been talking to her off and on the whole time we were eating. He was a little drunk and was with a large group of people, and he had taken a shine to this elegant, totally-in-control, woman.

He asked her what she did for a living. She looked at me, winked, and said to him, "I do janitorial work. I clean up other people's messes."

He wasn't at all put off. He told her he thought that must be interesting work. He wanted to know who she worked for. She said she worked for the state. She kept trying to ignore him and she was looking more frantic as the situation progressed.

When the waiter told her he'd paid for our dinner, she was beside herself. She looked at me with the most puzzled, shocked look on her face, and asked, "What should I do now? Should I offer to pay him back?"

I was delighted that she was so shook up. She could handle almost anything except a guy showing interest in her. I whispered, "Just thank him, and let's get out of here."

She did, and we left. She could be so normal and human, and then turn back into "the ruler," in control and out of reach. She was very assertive in her professional role. She could face down the governor if she thought it was important, but she didn't have a clue when it came to personal relationships, or at least that's the way it seemed.

I was thrilled to meet a niece and nephew of hers, both her sister Martha's children, several years ago, before I started this book. I spent several hours with the niece, who was wearing Ruby's turquoise dinner ring. The woman was a lovely 92-year-old, who physically resembled her aunt.

She told me about a totally different Ruby Miller who would come visit her sister in Tacoma once or twice a year. She said Ruby was playful, laughed a lot, took her and her brother places in Seattle, and was lots of fun, even for kids to be with. Maybe she wasn't all that different when I look back on it. She was a little more severe and serious in her professional life than with her family.

She told me about Ruby's father, who had been a railroad man. He had gotten trapped on a train track and had lost both of his hands when a train ran over them. That may have been where Ruby's affinity for wanting to take care of physically and emotionally crippled children came from.

She was very close to her sister, Martha. Whenever she was visiting, she took Criminology courses at the University of Washington in Seattle, and loved visiting the museums and art galleries there. She always took her niece and nephew with her and they told me she had a wonderful bizarre sense of humor.   I would have loved to have known that woman.

Her niece told me that Miss Miller came close to marriage twice. When she was Superintendent of the Choteau County School system in Montana, she had been involved with an alcoholic doctor in Great Falls. She finally got very angry about his drinking, walked into his office one day and threw the engagement ring on his desk. Then she walked out, keeping the pearl necklace he'd given her as a gift and that was the end of that.

Miss Miller told me once about a guy she got involved with when she was teaching in Augusta. The guy lived in New York and wanted her to come there and marry him. She said she got as far as to pack up and go to the train depot. A bunch of her students showed up there and they were crying. She couldn't bring herself to leave them, so she took her bags and went back home.

She went from being a teacher in Augusta, to being assistant assessor for Great Falls, to Superintendent of the Choteau Co. Schools, and finally to teaching math at the Girl's Vocational School, then, ultimately, the Administrator of the school. She never married.

I saw bits and pieces of her sense of humor, and her love of kids, but I do think, with her head poking through the "glass ceiling", she was much more on guard and feeling she had to be remote and strong at all times. Also, she was dealing with the prison system, and needed to keep her distance from the "inmates". I understand that more today than I did back then. A lot of the girls just thought she was a snooty bitch. She was far from being that.

What I experienced was a woman who would do very loving things, was deeply touched by kindness, and deeply hurt by meanness. She seemed to have no real knowledge of how to show feelings and sometimes seemed to be embarrassed by normal feelings. She had tremendous dignity and was very aristocratic, but I saw her cry too. And her anger was not to be challenged. She was a powerhouse in a knit suit.

Chapter 23

One of the excursions she took me on took place at a resort in Boulder, Montana. She told me to get ready and bring the flute along. We drove up a long lane, past Hereford cattle grazing, pine trees, and country fragrances. The place was tucked into the Cascade Mountains and it was lovely.

The resort was fancy, but not like the ones they have today. There was no swimming pool, or saunas, or massages. There were just rooms for the tourists, a fancy dining room, and a piano bar, with a guy playing soft music. All nestled in the a beautiful, mountainous countryside.

We had dinner after we left our things in the room. Ruby ordered prime rib for both of us. When the waiter brought the food, I couldn't believe she wanted me to eat that red bloody mess. I sat staring disgustedly at the meat and Miss Miller encouraged me to go ahead and try it.

Because I would have done anything for the woman and

frequently did, I took the first bite with my eyes closed. It melted in my mouth and I was hooked. The meat was so tender you could cut it with a fork and the taste was to die for. I don't even remember what we had for dessert. I just remember eating prime rib for the first time and loving it.

After dinner, Ruby had me go get my flute and meet her in the piano bar. I think my blood pressure went up a notch or two. I knew what she was going to ask me to do and I didn't know how to do it. I had no music with me and not a lot of musical training. I couldn't play by ear and was lost without sheet music.

The piano player must have wanted me to drop into a hole, as I fumbled around on the instrument, trying to follow what he was playing. I don't think, if he'd played "Mary Had a Little Lamb" I could have figured it out. Also, my bad hearing caused me problems, making it even worse. I had trouble distinguishing the notes. It was a nightmare and I finally admitted I just couldn't do it, gave up, and sat down.

I'm sure Miss Miller didn't understand music well enough to realize what was going on. She seemed to think that I was such a natural that I could play anything without music. Mrs. Giulio and the band teacher had taught me how to read music and had not taught me how to hear notes and be able to tell what they were. That would come much later and with a lot more playing and practice.

I didn't get "the look" however, when I sat back down. I think she realized she'd made a mistake and I was thoroughly humiliated. She never apologized, but I hope she appreciated my at least trying for her.

We spent the night there in a large attic room with twin beds. The next day we headed back to the school. The experience was interesting and fun, but stressful. I somehow felt I had let Miss Miller down, but there wasn't much I could do about it. It's an experience I'll never forget.

One afternoon I was playing the piano in the auditorium, and she came up to watch me. She asked me if I could teach her how to play. She said she used to play the drums and would like to know how to play the piano. I said I would and had her sit down. I tried to explain the notes on the piano to her. She got into an intellectual flurry and gave me a lot of grief over why the notes went a,b,c,d,e,f,g and then repeated. "Why didn't they go on down the alphabet?" she wanted to know.

Well, how the hell was I supposed to know? The question had never come up before. I didn't even ask questions like that. I tried to explain that they were easier to remember that way, because there were only seven notes to think about, but she wanted to change the whole system.

Looking back on it now, I think she was pulling my leg. Her sense of humor sometimes came out in very weird ways. I took the whole thing seriously then and got very exasperated with her. I tried to point out that it really didn't matter what she called them, as long as she learned where they were on the scale and understood the octaves. So then, she got into a major discussion with me about the octaves and why they were called that.

By the time the lesson was over, I wasn't sure I knew what octaves were! She then told me she should probably just stick to playing drums, because she wasn't cut out to play the piano. She turned and left to go back downstairs, but not before I noticed a silly grin cross her face. I just shook my head and went back to practicing.

There was a full-size accordion behind the stage curtain in the auditorium where the instruments were kept. I decided I needed to learn to play it. I had some knowledge of all the wind instruments and could play a couple of them, besides the flute, fairly well. Mrs. Giulio never could understand my need to play anything but the piano and the flute. I just loved challenging myself with these instruments.

After I learned to play the bugle a little, Miss Miller had me play taps one morning while we raised the flag. I passed out and she never asked me to do that again. I guess I just didn't have the breathing down very well.

Anyway, Mr. Porter started giving me lessons on the accordion. I'd been playing for about six weeks, when Miss Miller did it to me again. She decided I should perform for the Soroptomist Club in Helena. I told her I didn't think I was ready, but she thought I was, and that was that.

So, Mrs. Giulio put together a music program and off we went - the chorus, Carol, and me. Carol was the master of ceremonies. We sang some songs and then she announced me and I stood up with that accordion.

Strangely, I wasn't nervous. I rarely got nervous during these things. I didn't really relate to success or failure. I just did what I was asked to do. I knew I was over-stepping my ability with the accordion, but, hey, what the heck. I'd give it a shot.

I started playing a march I'd learned that had a lot of bass in it. Everything was going well, until about half way through the piece, I had a brain blip and the rest of the piece just left me. I stopped, looked out at the women watching me stumble around and said, "Sorry ladies. That's all she wrote."

I looked at the back of the room where Miss Miller sat, and she had "that look" on her face. It was a combination of disapproval, disgust, and "I'm going to kill you when I get you home." I smiled at her, shrugged, put the instrument down, and sat back down with the chorus.

Carol came to my rescue. She spoke into the stunned silence of the room with her booming voice. "Well, I think Helen did a pretty good job for only having learned that instrument six weeks ago. Let's give her a round of applause for effort."

The women all dutifully applauded. Later in the program, I played the piano for them, and they loved it. I played a flute solo for them as well and they totally forgave the accordion debacle.

Chapter 24

It turned out that Miss Miller was trying to get these club members to pay for me to go to the University of Montana in Missoula for a week-long music camp. I think they must have agreed, because that's where I wound up that summer.

She and I went on a shopping trip to the Bon Marche. She bought me several "outside" outfits, including underwear, and a thing they called a "Merry Widow". It was an undergarment that tightened your waistline and gave you cleavage. Why she thought I needed that, I have no idea. But I wore the thing and it gave me an hourglass figure. I was heavier than I'd ever been when I was at the school and everybody was into having a small Scarlet O'Hara waist, unlike later, when they want you to be just plain thin with the bones standing out. Even Marilyn Monroe would be considered too heavy in 70's fashion expectations. Now they want women to look healthy. It's about time!

Miss Miller and I had a great time shopping for clothes like a couple of teen-age girls. She picked out a skirt with the new rage Elvis Presley plastered all over it, along with his guitar. I wasn't sure that was going to fit into a classical music camp, but I agreed to it, and did actually wear it once. I got some pretty odd looks. She even bought me a can-can slip to wear under it. Style was the name of the game and she was going to send me off in style!

I was trying to project the image of intellectual snobbery and the Elvis skirt just didn't fit into that image. I guess I didn't really fit into it either. I didn't quite understand what the life background had to entail to develop that image, but I tried. A little reform school girl with an incredibly neglected background trying to fit into this "rich kid's" world, seems ludicrous to me now, but my mentor believed I could do it, so I tried.

I did okay, I guess. As soon as Arlette got me settled in the college dorm and was gone, I knew I wasn't going to fit in. I had no idea what to do, what to say, or why I was even there. I did have a couple of girls who hung out with me a little, so I wasn't totally lonely.

I knew one of the girls who was there, from the days with Joe the farm hand. Her name was Irene. She was the daughter of the farmer whose place Joe and my mother were working on when we lived in Fort Benton.

The parents had a house in town, right across from the grade school. Irene was an only child and she was absolutely adored. She also played the flute, but had had professional lessons and played circles around me. She remembered me enough to say hello, but really didn't want anything to do with me. She was way out of my league. I had no idea how to relate to her.

Some of the music camp was fun. The conductor of the Helena Symphony Orchestra was head of the music festival and he conducted the orchestra and the band that week. Miss Miller had set it up for me to take a flute lesson from him. The lessons were interesting. He taught me how to breathe. I was wearing a big wide, tight-fitting belt around my waists to emphasize the tiny circumference, plus the Merry Widow. It was style. Of course, it shoved my lungs nearly up into my throat.

The first thing he said was, "Unbuckle that thing." Reluctantly, I did as I was told and he taught me how to fill my lungs with air. It sure made a difference in the playing. After the lesson he pointed out to me that I really didn't have the technique for the band.

Band music is usually fast paced and has lots of runs in it for the flute. I suffered horribly during band practice, trying to keep up and failing. He blessed me by saying, "You're in chorus, orchestra, and the choir. Why don't you just forget about band and do those things?"

I was so grateful for that, even though I was a little embarrassed. I hadn't signed up for all that stuff. Miss Miller signed me up for it. I knew she would not be happy, but I sure was. I was way over my head with the band. Even the orchestra was rough, but I was used to playing orchestra music and managed to hold my own without ruining the sound.

The little girl that played the concerto with the Helena Symphony was there. She lived in Missoula and of course, attended the music camp every year. Surprisingly, she was playing the kettle drums in the orchestra and she sure looked like she was having fun. Her sister played first violin. I didn't know it then, but she also sang opera, and as I said before, wound up singing at the Metropolitan Opera as an adult.

The week was fun and went by fairly fast, but it was stressful too. I tried to fit in and, I guess did okay, but I was glad when it was over. I, of course, embarrassed myself by dancing down the hall in the dorm, singing happily that I was going home.

The kids probably thought I was crazy, but I just didn't care. I was happy to have a home to go to. The school and Miss Miller were the only security I'd ever known.

Miss Miller wasn't happy about me being asked to drop out of the band. I told her it was as much my idea as it was the conductors. I wasn't doing well and it was embarrassing. She just couldn't get it that there were some things I just couldn't do. I wasn't well enough trained for some of her expectations.

She didn't come for the concerts. And Arlette came to get me and take me home. That was a disappointment, but I didn't have a lot of expectations of Miss Miller. I just took things as they came, usually.

Another time, I came into the Administration building and went up to the auditorium to play the piano for a while. There, much to my delight sat a little organ. Of course, I sat down, turned it on and began to play with it. I spent hours playing that thing and had a wonderful time with it.

The little instrument lived there at the back of the auditorium for about two weeks, when I was approached by Miss Miller and the priest who did mass on Sunday mornings. I played the piano for the church services on Sundays and always picked out the music that would be sung during the service. I guess these two thought it would be a great idea if I would play the organ for mass at six o'clock in the morning as well.

They approached me with the request. Then, I got the picture. That's why the organ was sitting there. It was a hook. I told them no, not because I minded playing for the mass, but I didn't want to get up that early on a Sunday morning. Needless to say, the organ disappeared the next day. Probably back into the Catholic Church. I heard no more about playing mass after that.

Chapter 25

I got spanked twice while I was at the school. Both times by Miss Miller and both times with a ping-pong paddle. I don't know where that paddle came from. There wasn't a ping- pong table in sight anywhere.

Once, early on in my days there, she lined several of us girls up in the piano room and gave us each a pretty good swat with that thing. What we did was considered a no-no by the staff and it had to have been pretty serious to have her come over and give us each a swat with the paddle. It didn't hurt much, just embarrassed everybody.

It had to do with the dinner table. One of the girls and I got into a stare-down, and wouldn't leave when we were told to. I'm thinking the other girls wouldn't leave because they wanted to see who won. Teen-age thinking--!

The second time, I was really spanked. I was maybe sixteen and still a little street kiddish. What happened was, one of the girls and I got into yet another staring match at the dinner table. Neither one of us was going to be the first one to give way and drop our eyes. It wasn't an aggressive duel, just who could keep the stare going the longest.

Mrs. Mackey, "Gutsa", was the matron on duty. Gutsa couldn't have been over four feet, six inches tall. She had dark hair, very little gray in it, worn short and curled. She was in her fifties, with a stern little face, beady dark eyes, and very controlling. She liked to show her displeasure by standing with her hands on her hips, and screwing her little face into a dark scowl. She could look pretty formidable at times, and she rarely smiled.

She stood over us, hands on hips, insisting that we leave the table, and when we didn't respond, she grabbed my arm and tried to pull me out of the chair. I got angry and called her a bitch.

She led me away from the table and into the matron's sitting room in the back of the building. I didn't fight her, but I was sure pissed off. I think the woman kind of reminded me of my mother.

When she got me to the pretty, well-decorated, little sitting room, she made me sit on the floor and went to call Miss Miller. I didn't care. I was mad and I didn't think the behavior called for the roughness.

I think some of the matrons, and the office staff, were more jealous of my feelings for Miss Miller than any of the girls ever were. Gutsa seemed very pleased with herself to be getting me into trouble. She could put a nasty grin on her face that made you want to slap her.

Sitting on the floor, back against the wall, I looked up from staring at the floor, and feeling very sorry for myself, and there stood my mentor, filling the French doorway with her presence, and she didn't look happy.

When she was angry, her brow would furrow, her thin lips would be tightly pressed together, and you could hardly see her mouth. She would put "the look" on her face and your blood would go cold. Nobody had any doubt they were in deep trouble when they saw that look.

Gutsa stood behind the angry woman, little hands on her hips, and a triumphant look on her face.

"What do you think you're doing calling Mrs. Mackey a bitch?" Miss Miller asked me in a very strained, tight-lipped voice.

I answered her, all the time staring at the little woman standing there grinning. "Well, tell her to quit acting like a bitch and I won't call her one."

Wrong answer! Without another word, Miss Miller took me by the arm and led me into the other matron's sitting room. This room was right across the entry to the girls' living room. She closed the door. In her hand, she held the ping-pong paddle, and she used it on me. She didn't hit me hard, but it still stung. I'm sure there were girls outside the door counting.

After the paddling, she sent me up to my room. I went upstairs, crawled into my bed, and cried. She came up later and checked on me, then she left. I realized later that I wasn't crying because the spanking hurt, or that I was humiliated. I was crying because I had never had anyone care enough about me to discipline me like that. I guess, at that point, I really felt that Miss Miller loved, and cared about me.

It amazes me that I didn't connect love and hitting, from that situation. I had promised myself years ago, because of the situation with my mother and Joe, I would never put up with anyone hitting me. And I never have. But that situation with Ruby was not meant to be a mean act, or even meant to hurt me. It was how they disciplined in those days, and tried to teach obedience.

Miss Miller was a very gentle soul and I knew she'd never deliberately hurt me. She couldn't let me get away with things like that, or the other girls would expect to get away with it too, and it would put the matrons in danger. Also, allowing me to get away with it could have put me in danger as well.

I think that's why she moved the spanking to within earshot of the other girls. I didn't try to fight back. I would have never threatened this woman, even if she'd have beaten me to death. And, looking back, I deserved the spanking. There were probably other incidents where I should have been spanked and wasn't.

I think Gutsa was a bit of a closet drunk. Very late one night, she came home to the cottage and was very drunk. She fell trying to stagger up the stairs to her room and wound up crawling on her hands and knees. She crawled, drunkenly, down the hall, past the night matron, and into her room. The night matron, evidently, just watched, and never offered her any help. We girls all thought this was pretty funny.

I don't know if Gutsa ever got into trouble over that incident. I sure hope she did. At least, to my knowledge, it never happened again. She probably kept her drinking in her room from then on.

Mrs. Flannigan was the head matron in Canady Hall. She was maybe in her sixties, if not older, five foot seven, a hundred sixty pounds, gray/blonde hair, and another mean one. She had been a matron at the school for many years and went from being the girl's pal, and sharing dirty jokes with them, to being nasty and cruel with her mouth, sometimes all within the same ten or fifteen minutes. She, too, was a bit of a control freak and wasn't well-liked.

One time she told me a joke about Liberace and his mother. I didn't understand the joke, but, in my naiveté, I thought Miss Miller would enjoy it, because Mrs. Flannigan seemed to think it was funny. Miss Miller was not amused and Mrs. Flannigan never shared another one of her jokes with me.

As a matter of fact, she wasn't very enamored with me after that. I had no idea what I'd done wrong. The joke had to do with Liberace being told to go back where he came from and he tried to take his piano.

Mrs. Flannigan used to like to talk about being the first woman to ever see the Lewis and Clark Caverns. When it was discovered, it was a big hole in the ground and the only way in was to be lowered down by rope. She was the first woman to ever venture into the caverns that way. I thought that was pretty cool, if it was true, and I never doubted it. She was a tough old bird.

This lady could be abusive, and often was. One day she got mad at a couple of the girls for some reason and made them sit in the living room during supper, without eating. After dinner, she made them do the dishes over and over. Then she sent them to bed. I'm not sure what they had done to set her off, but her punishment was mean and uncalled- for. She really liked the power she had over us.

She also liked to make fun of the girls and call them names. I know she was aware of what was going on when those girls were scrubbing down the little girl with the scrub brushes and she did nothing to stop it. She was the one on duty at the time and the matrons always knew what was going on. If they didn't, someone would tell them. It's interesting how a place like that will draw some really sadistic people. She was instrumental in getting rid of several people that the girls really liked. Jealousy, maybe, I don't know.

There was a woman who came to work at Canady Hall as a cook, who had just been paroled from the prison in Deer Lodge. She was fortyish, nice, scared to death, and a lousy cook. She wasn't scared of the girls, just scared of failing.

We all tried really hard to help her keep her job. Some of the girls who worked in the kitchen tried to teach the woman to cook, but she wasn't cut out for that sort of work. We tried to suffer out the bad food, but Mrs. Flannigan would say snide things to the woman, and worked hard to get her fired. Even though the kitchen girls and the breakfast/lunch cook offered to help her, Mrs. Flannigan finally talked Miss Miller into getting rid of the woman. She cried when she left and I really hope she found another situation to work in that wasn't so stressful. She was a nice lady.

Things got so bad with this matron that the girls all got together and asked me and two other girls to go talk to Miss Miller about it. They thought she would listen to me, and maybe get Flannigan to back off a little.

We asked for a meeting with our Superintendent and she agreed, not knowing what it was about. She sat and listened to our complaints, tight-lipped, and angry. Then she said, "How dare you come in here complaining about one of my matrons. I'm not going to listen to any more of this. You girls go back home and give some thought to what you might do to prevent her from getting so rough with you again." And that was the end of the meeting. So much for the rights of the masses!

We girls left mumbling to each other about the unfairness of it all. However, not only did Mrs. Flannigan stop doing what she was doing, but she soon left Canady Hall and was never seen again by us girls. Who knows what happened. I assumed she was sent to some other job in the state, or she retired. I guess Miss Miller heard us after all. She just needed to do some investigating of her own and didn't want us to think all we had to do was pitch a gripe and she'd kick out whoever we didn't happen to like. One thing I know for sure. She didn't tolerate abuse of her girls well.

The only thing I missed about Flannigan was her boiled dinners on Thursday nights. She made a dynamite pot roast.

Chapter 26

In early 1957 things began to change at the school. Some really rough girls were being sent to there for breaking some very serious laws. The first ones to come in were two sisters. For some reason, they were put into Canady Hall together and they immediately became the alpha females in the cottage.

They had been picked up for prostitution, and were sent to the school to get them off the streets. They were not the typical girls that came in out there. Penny was the oldest. She was a pretty, five-foot-six-inch girl, well built, with reddish-blonde hair that was cut to lie around her slender neck, and frame her face. She liked running the show and most of the other girls were awed by, and afraid of, her and her sister.

Her sister was kind of like a bodyguard. She was bigger than Penny, heavy, and not nearly as smart. But she was more physically mean than her big sister. Penny was intellectually mean and thought up the nasty stuff that her sister carried through on.

Cindy was not a pretty girl. She had beautiful German skin and naturally curly blonde hair, but her face was too round, and her eyes were too small to be pretty. Attitude just dripped off her. She was maybe fourteen or fifteen, her sister being close to seventeen. She pushed everybody around and totally idolized her big sister. Nobody got in Cindy's way.

Penny taught several of us girls to do the jitterbug steps. We'd line up behind her in the living room, hands on one another's hips, and follow her steps around the room. She was a very good dancer and I later found out that she could paint really well. I sure hope she did something with that talent when she quit raising hell.

One night I was sitting in the living room, reading my ever-present Bible. There were several girls in the room and I wasn't paying attention to any of them. I sensed something was up, looked up, and there were five or six girls gathered around my chair, including Cindy, being egged on by Penny. I'd not had too many really bad experiences with the girls out there, so I didn't have my guard up.

Penny looked at me with a sneer on her face and said, "Hey, how do you think God is going to help you out of this one?"

I looked at her confused and, knowing this was serious stuff, I surprised myself with what came out of my mouth. I said, "I don't know what you're talking about. What did I do to piss you off?"

"Everything about you pisses me off," she said softly. Then, with no warning, Cindy and a couple of the other girls grabbed me and held me down. Penny, wielding a broom, took aim, while two other girls tried to pull my legs apart. She was going to rape me with that broom. My dress was up around my neck and they were going for my panties.

I look back on that today and wonder that I didn't get angry and go berserk. Instead, I closed my eyes and said out loud, "Oh, God! Forgive them for they don't know what they are doing." To this day I have no idea where that came from, or why I said it. It doesn't seem to be one of the most appropriate reactions to a situation like that.

However, to my surprise and relief, they turned me loose immediately. I didn't question anything. I got up and ran out of the room and up the stairs leading to the girls' bedrooms. The door was locked, so I sat on the stairs and cried in anger and humiliation.

There was a little eleven-year-old girl named Yvonne, who had come in with her two sisters. One of them had been put into Maria Dean and she'd been sent to Canady Hall along with the oldest of the three. They never should have been separated from each other, let alone put into a place like that. They hadn't done anything other than be unwanted.

Anyhow, this wonderful little girl came creeping up the stairs and touched my knee. I looked at her through my tears and she said, "I'm really sorry, Helen." I smiled and thanked her.

Cindy came out of the living room at that moment and said to the little girl in a threatening voice, "If you know what's good for you, you'd better get away from her."

Yvonne, sensibly, looked scared and went back down the stairs and into the living room. I'll never forget the compassion that that brave little girl showed for me that night. None of the girls ever bothered me again after that. I think they thought I had some special "in" with God, or maybe they thought I was a witch. Whatever their superstitions told them about me, I was grateful, because they left me alone.

I really did try to fit in with the other girls. Sometimes I hurt people by trying to go along with some of the stuff they did.

We got a new night matron. She was naïve about kids like us, and a little scared. The girls constantly said things to her that she thought was polite banter, but was really sarcastic and nasty comments, made to make her look foolish. She didn't catch the disdainful nuances connected with what they were saying and doing. This was not a good place for someone to work who was naïve about, or afraid of, these girls.

I'm ashamed to admit that I did my share of trying to make this woman look foolish also. One night, while we were getting ready for bed, I decided to have some fun with the matron. I went to her, flanked by a couple of my cohorts and asked, "Mrs. Stone. Where do babies come from?"

She looked at me flustered and shocked by the question. She said, "I don't think we should be talking about such things."

I said, without batting an eye, or giggling, "These girls are telling me that if you swallow a watermelon seed it will make a baby. Is that true?"

The poor woman was so shaken and embarrassed that she blushed. Believe it or not, she actually said to me, "Helen, I don't know." I couldn't believe she said that. The other two girls started walking away in fits of giggling. Me, I wouldn't leave it alone.

I asked, "Don't you have kids?" She nodded, yes. I asked, "Did you swallow watermelon seeds to get them?"

She blanched and did the only thing she appeared to be able to think of to do. She mumbled something about needing to make rounds and check on the other girls, got up from her chair and walked away, leaving me nearly rolling on the floor, holding my sides in stitches of laughter.

Six months later, this same matron was attacked. There was a plan brewing among some of the girls, being led by Penny and Cindy. I heard snippets of it, but didn't know too much. A group of about six girls were planning a breakout in the middle of the night. I didn't say anything to Miss Miller because I had no intention of being a snitch and living in hell for the rest of the time I was there.

Of course, I didn't know the whole story, of what they were planning, or I may have said something. My roommate and I had a room behind the matron's chair at the time. We knew this thing was going down that night and we lay in our beds, waiting.

Suddenly, we heard shuffling. The matron said, "What are you girls doing. Go back to your rooms." We heard a loud "thunk" noise, then another and another. Then she screamed and begged and cried, and she was silent. Chubby, my little roommate and friend, and I crawled into bed together and held onto each other. We were scared to death and helpless to do anything. We just lay there together and listened to the rustling in the hallway.

We heard the upstairs door being unlocked, and then silence. Chubby went back to her own bed and we waited. The sounds of feet running back up the stairs, through the halls, then, silence again.

Apparently they couldn't get the front door open and they saw Miss Miller coming down the walkway with reinforcements before they could find the right key.

She came upstairs, followed by two of the maintenance men, then sirens, as the police, and an ambulance, pulled up outside. They searched every room but ours. When one of the officers started back for our room, I heard Miss Miller say, "No, those girls would not have been involved. You don't need to go there." And they didn't.

Every girl who had clothing thrown on her closet floor was suspect and was taken to jail. Some of the girls were in bed with their clothes still on. One of the girls, who wasn't involved, but so wanted to be included, actually gave herself up and claimed she'd been involved. So, they took her too. She wasn't a bad girl, just slow and very lost. I'm sure she regretted her decision later.

We learned the next day that Cindy had beaten poor Mrs. Stone on the head with a statue of the Madonna, for God's sake. They'd taken her keys and got as far as the front door when they saw Miss Miller and two big men coming up the stairs to the cottage. Gutsa had called the main office from her room next to the matron's chair and they'd come running.

The six girls were taken to jail in Helena, where Penny and Cindy entertained themselves by stripping naked and dancing for bystanders in front of the upstairs window of their cell. Finally, when they got tired of being locked up, they plugged up the toilet and flooded their cell.

This didn't get them anything but a cleanup job. Then they forced soapy water down the throat of the poor unfortunate little girl who'd wanted to be a part of their crowd. When she threw her guts up, they screamed for the jailer, who, stupidly, opened the cell door to help the little girl. He was promptly beaten to a pulp and his keys taken. The girls then locked him up in his own jail, and they were off to new, more exciting adventure.

The sheriff's apartment was in the jail. The jail breakers ran through it, scaring the hell out of the sheriff's wife. Down the stairs and out the door they went, throwing the jailer's keys all over the streets as they ran. I don't know how far they got, but none of them ever came back to the school.

A month or so later, Penny was begging to be allowed back,

and Miss Miller said no way. I don't know where she landed, but she sent Miss Miller one of her paintings, and I understand it was quite good. I'm sure GVS was heaven compared to wherever those two sisters wound up. They more than likely ended up in the women's ward at the state prison in Deer Lodge. I sure didn't have any sympathy for them.

I later was going to feel some of the brunt of this escapade by these girls. What they did was how the girls from the school were ultimately judged by the "outside" world. Sad but true. The matron never came back to the school when she got out of the hospital. We never heard how badly she was hurt.

Miss Miller was a wreck the next morning. She just couldn't believe that something like that could happen in her school. She kept saying, "They beat the poor woman with a statue of the Madonna," and shaking her head in disbelief. I always felt a little guilty that I hadn't warned her about what was coming, but, I too, had to make some choices.

If I'd have ratted on those girls, I'm not sure what would have happened to me, but I don't think it would have been pretty. I hope if

I'd have known what the full plan was, that I would have taken the risk and told someone. I had no idea they were going to hurt the matron and I'm not sure anybody else did either. Everyone knew about the escape plan, but I'm not sure anyone knew that Cindy was going to try to beat the woman to death. It was a relief to have these girls gone.

Chapter 27

During the summer, a lot of the girls would go home, and come back in the fall. They also got to go home for Christmas. I had no place to go during the summer most of the time, and no desire to leave anyway. So I went to summer school and played softball.

GVS had a softball team that was pretty lousy, but fun. A couple of the girls were pretty good and could have played on a much better women's team, but we, as a whole, were pretty bad.

We would break up into two teams and I would play catcher on mine. The batters would complain that I squatted too close to the batters' box and made them nervous. That was the whole idea. I always caught my ball.

Mrs. Giulio was concerned that I was going to injure my hands and not be able to play the piano and the flute. I just laughed and told her I'd be fine, and I was.

There was a woman that worked as an assistant to Ruby at the school. She was probably mid-thirties and very athletic. She was our softball coach. She played on a team in Helena called the Days. They were the top women's softball team in the state at that time.

Loreen actually talked these wonderful women into coming out to the school and playing a game with our team. We got slaughtered by them and they barely lifted a finger or broke a sweat as they ran us into the ground. However, they did allow us to make one run. And I was the lucky one that got to make it.

I made a hit at bat, and the women at the bases actually prompted me when to run. They let me get the one run in and then they creamed us. It was wonderful fun and a real privilege to get to play this team.

That same summer Miss Miller was out watching us play one day. After the game we were hanging around her, talking. She asked us something about where Yellowstone Park was located. I said I thought it was in England somewhere and nobody else had an answer. She decided that Montana History was going to be one of the subjects taught that summer. I wasn't very popular after that, but we sure learned a lot about Montana.

Anything the girls wanted to learn at the school, Ruby was ready to set it up. She had a beauty culture class, cooking classes, typing classes, anything she could think of besides the required curriculum for the state, to try and help the girls get a leg up on the outside world. We all did a stint in the laundry on Saturday mornings to learn how to handle laundry machines. After all, this was supposed to be the "Vocational School".

The laundry was in the basement of the Administration

building. Every Saturday morning, we girls that worked there would line up, be counted, and head for the main building.

I took my turn at working on the mangle, a huge roller that was used to press sheets, and flat stuff. It took two people to feed it and two to catch the items at the other end. We'd stand feeding sheets into the big white roller, and telling stories about people getting their arms or hair caught up in it. They were bloody stories, chock full of body parts, and lots of pain, and screaming. It was pretty gruesome and fun, scaring the hell out of ourselves. And woe be it to the new girl on the mangle. She'd have nightmares for weeks by the time she was filled with the horror stories.

I never did get a job in a laundry, as an adult. I did, however, work as a typist for a while in an insurance company, so the typing class came in handy. Miss Miller got me that job, which we'll cover later.

That summer we put on a little fair in the little park in front of the Administration Building. I remember very little about it. There was lots of good food, games to play, and Arlette gave rides in her old antique Whippet, which she kept in perfect condition all the time.

Miss Miller sent me to my mother three times while I was in the school. I didn't ask to go see her, I was told I would be going and I went. The first time, she was working on a wheat farm outside of Great Falls. I was maybe fifteen. Mom was cooking for the farmer. I lasted there nearly a week.

I went back to trying to be somebody's little girl and got myself into trouble. I followed the farm hand around, watching him work. He reminded me of Joe, and was probably the same age. One day, we were in the grain silo and I was sliding down the grain. I had a dress on because that's what I had for clothing.

I guess I wasn't paying close attention, because the next thing I knew, the guy was looking lecherously at me. He said, "What would you do if I decided to rape you?"

I said something stupid, like, "If you're going to talk that way, I'm leaving," and I did. I took off across the field and he came after me on a tractor. I managed to hide from him and, to this day, I don't remember how I got back to the school. I think I went back to the farm house and my mother accused me of coming on to the guy. I knew she and he were sleeping together and I was astonished that he would tell her something like that.

Anyway, she lost her job and I wound up back at the school, which I didn't consider punishment.

The second time, my mother was living in Great Falls in a downtown hotel. It was maybe Easter and I was sixteen. I met up with the little girl I'd known when I was three or four; the one whose mom played the piano.

We hung out for a while during that visit. Glenda was living with her dad, and her mom was on the streets of Great Falls, deeply into her alcoholism. She'd go into the bars and play the piano for drinks. Glenda's dad would bring her back to their house when he could get her to come, and they'd try to dry her out and clean her up.

The woman had been a beautiful lady once. She'd had tuberculosis when she was younger and had a lot of scars on her neck. She always wore a pretty silk scarf around her neck to cover the scars. Even in her drunkest years, she kept the scars covered. Strange what becomes important to people no matter what.

During that visit I met a guy, of course, three times my age, who decided to take me on as a girl friend. He never got sexual with me, but I hung out with him and his friends most of the time I was in Great Falls.

Miss Miller would have had a conniption fit if she'd have known about the life I went into when she sent me to be with my mother. I think she might have put a stop to it, had she known. Maybe she did, especially after the last visit.

The last time I was sent to be with my mother was a Christmas holiday. I was still sixteen, didn't want to go, and was forced into it. Ruby didn't like my digging heels in and I always gave in.

My mother was in Helena at the time working at the Placer Hotel as an elevator operator. The hotel was owned by one of the richest men in the state, a lawyer by the name of Rankin.

He and my mother's uncle had been involved in some shenanigans in the past. My mother's uncle had worked for Anaconda Copper and was very powerful politically. Mr. Rankin was somehow mixed up with him. Mom's uncle eventually got himself into so much political hot water that he was run out of the state. I'm pretty sure that's how Mr. Rankin knew my mother and why he hired her at the hotel.

Arlette dropped me off at the hotel. I was very sick and really didn't want to be there. I tried to get my mother to give me her keys so I could go to her apartment and lie down, but she refused. Probably thought I'd rob her or something. Anyhow, I suffered through her shift and we finally went to her place.

She lived in the basement of a big house. A woman and her boyfriend lived on the main floor. The woman had this beautiful, dark-haired, black-eyed little four-year-old son that just took your breath away, he was so cute. And, he was a good kid. Quiet, never causing her any trouble, but, the boyfriend didn't like him. So she put him in an orphanage so she could keep the boyfriend. Even now when I read this it makes me cry.

I never forgot that little boy and how totally shocked I was that she would give him up for that scumbag. I guess I could relate. My mother did crap like that to me all the time. It still makes me angry when I think about that little kid and I wonder, sometimes, whatever happened to him.   I hope he grew up to be wonderful and successful in spite of a useless mother.

I'll guarantee you, as a counselor in later years, any woman in that same situation, heard the story of that little boy. I've never understood giving up your kids for a boyfriend.

Anyhow, I regress. I laid around my mother's apartment for the rest of the day and into the evening, getting sicker and sicker. I stayed all of the next day and, when my mother went to work late that afternoon, I left. It was Christmas Eve.

It was the middle of winter in Montana, snow on the ground, and cold. I decided to walk back to the school which was about eight or ten miles from town. Nobody ever ran away from home and back to reform school, so, I think, I may have made history that night.

It was a cold, clear, star-filled night. The snow reflected the moonlight and the whole world was encompassed in a brilliant glow. It was beautiful and miserable. I was not appreciative of the glory of it all. I was sick, cold, wet, and wanted to be home in my own bed.

I walked across the railroad yard on the edge of town and found the valley highway. I walked along the side of the road, never thinking to try and hitch a ride, never thinking to call the school, just putting one foot in front of the other.

I was feverish and wasn't thinking clearly. It never occurred to me that I could freeze to death out there. I had my warm "Pea" coat, gloves, a scarf, and boots, and I was doing pretty well the first five miles. Things got rougher, I got colder.

There wasn't much traffic on the highway because of the icy road, the lateness, and the holiday. It was getting along about two in the morning. I was getting tired and very cold, and coughing more and more.

I finally gave up, and went to a house near the highway. They didn't have fences and stone walls to block the traffic noise back then, so I just walked up a driveway and began ringing the doorbell.

A woman came to the door and I told her who I was and asked her to call Miss Miller. She brought me into her house, fussing over me, and called the school. It took Miss Miller about fifteen minutes to show up at the woman's door to get me.

She drove me back to the school, bawling me out for not calling her from town, instead of trying to walk it. She put me to bed in her guest room and gave me hot cocoa. The next morning, I was taken to the cottage, put to bed, and a doctor was called. I don't remember the next three days. I remember being given little red pills, frequently, but that's it. I was very, very sick, but I'd made it home. That was the last time she tried to make me go to visit my mother.

My mother came to see me three times. Once, to get my watch to pawn and once to bring the dog, Trixie out for Arlette to take care of. I have no idea how that all took place. But the dog was pregnant and wound up having five puppies. It was the strangest thing to see that little dog walking across the grounds with all those puppies bouncing through the snow behind her.

Miss Miller fought her way through a snowstorm to take my mother back to town the night she brought the dog. I don't why she was so adamant to get rid of her, but she was. I think my mother thought she could stay there too and we could all live happily ever after. She wanted to be taken care of and couldn't find a guy to do it.

The third time the woman showed up, she was on her way to Billings to have an abortion. It seems she was living with a guy in Great Falls and got pregnant. He really didn't want any kids with her, so he sent her off to a doctor in Billings to take care of it. Why she needed to stop by and tell me about it is a mystery. She never got over seeing me as her girlfriend, I guess. Needless to say, I was never thrilled to see her coming. She always meant trouble when she showed up.

I think, by now, Miss Miller was getting the picture of my lifestyle with my mother. She stopped trying to patch up the relationship and started thinking about what was going to become of me when I left the school.

Chapter 28

The math teacher quit when I was a sophomore. Why, I don't know, but she did, right in the middle of the school year. She probably found a less stressful place to teach and grabbed it. It's not easy to work in a place like GVS, even though back then the kids weren't that rough. There weren't the drugs - just drinking and boyfriends and bad parenting.

I don't know how hard it was to find substitute teachers, but we had a string of them. We girls prided ourselves on how quickly we could run these subs off. It really didn't take much. One thing that none of these poor women got right was, you never walk into a place like that showing fear. People in incarcerated situations can smell fear and all it does is excite them. We, even though we were young girls, were no different.

Fear just brought out the animal in us and we couldn't help ourselves. We never hurt any of them, but we did terrorize them. They had good reason to be afraid by the time they left.

The torture would start with the class walking into the room and everybody sitting in the wrong seats and going by the wrong names during roll call. I had that pulled on me when I was student teaching in Missoula. It's confusing and frustrating watching the kids snigger into their hands.

Girls would get up and wander around the room, talk to each other, and just flat walk out of the classroom, while the teacher was trying to explain a math problem. Some of them would just sit and glare at the poor soul.

I didn't have much sympathy for these women either. I did my own little messing with them, thinking it was pretty funny. There's something about being a teen-ager and knowing people are afraid of you that gives you a sense of power. At least it did me.

My contribution to the terror was to go up behind the teachers and pound eraser dust into their hair. I know they could hear the eraser and knew someone was behind them, but, incredibly, they never turned around to find out what was going on.

I would have never physically hurt one of them and I don't think any of the other girls would have either, but we sure scared the hell out of them. They didn't realize we wouldn't hurt them and that they could have called Miss Miller, or Arlette at any time, and all hell would have broken loose. They didn't. They just didn't show up the next day. Our score was three up and three down. We were proud. However, there was a price to pay for our antics.

Miss Miller gave up when the third substitute walked out before the school day was over. She came into the classroom and announced that she was going to finish out the math course and we'd better all pass with a very good grade. She had been a math major with a minor in art, so she knew what she was doing. We all came out with an A for the class and she proved to be a very patient and knowledgeable teacher. I think she enjoyed herself and we really got a lot out of the class.

On the other hand, these same girls would go to the wire for someone they could relate to, as I said before.

We had a wonderful English teacher by the name of Mrs.

Fredrigill. She was probably mid-forties. Age is hard to judge when you're a teen. She was short, had a wonderful hourglass figure, dark hair, dark eyes, and a quick smile. In this day and age, as women of that age are judged, she would have been considered quite sexy, even though she didn't try to project that image.

I know nothing about her personal life. She was probably married and had some kids, but I don't know for sure. As a teacher, she was one of the best. She developed a love in me for literature and poetry, and she too was into theater.

I don't know if they still do, but back then the states had oratory contests once a year. They included declamations which could be humorous, dramatic, or oratorical. I think they may have had debate teams as well from the different schools. Mrs. Fredrigill liked to get the girls that could do public speaking involved in these speech meets.

We would practice for months until we had them down pat, and off we'd go to one of the colleges to give our declamation. Miss Miller always liked to go along and root us on.

The first year I got involved, I did a thing called, "Sixteen" by

Maureen Daly. It was a monologue about a teen-age girl who had just had her first date and was hovering over the phone in agony, wondering if the guy would call her again.

We would perform our speeches in front of all the girls in the school to get the feel of an audience, but, also, because they liked to hear them.

I did okay with "Sixteen", but it never did go anywhere. Monologues weren't very popular at the meets no matter how well they were done, because they couldn't stand up to a declamation that had a lot of different characters in it. The trip was fun though.

I don't remember where we went the first time I gave that declamation, but, the next year, the meet was held in Bozeman at Montana State University.

The second year, I took "Sixteen" again, and decided I wanted to do a humorous one as well. I learned a thing called, "The Speech Judge's Nightmare". It was a wonderful declamation about a speech judge who dreamed bits and pieces of a bunch of declamations he'd judged that day.

Mrs. Fredrigill and I worked and worked on that declamation.

I really had it down well and could send her into peals of laughter, even after she'd heard it several times. We both just knew I was going to place with that performance.

Carol and Sarah also learned declamations and we were all going to Bozeman to compete. I was excited. We all were.

The kids at Canady Hall asked me to give the speech for them one night. One of the characters was a man in a cell scheduled to be executed. He went on and on about his terror of the whole process, and then he screamed out in a pleading voice, "What time is it? What time is it?"

Gutsa's voice rang out in response from the hall. "It's eight o'clock."

We all fell apart, but I swallowed my hilarity and managed to keep going. It was a fun night and I felt really good about performing this thing. The next day, we gave the declamations for the whole school.

My declamation included a woman trying to get into a corset, an opera singer, the condemned man, and several other rather loud raucous characters. As I rampaged around the front of the auditorium, I looked at the back of the room. Mrs. Fredrigill was grinning from ear to ear, pride literally dripping off her face and Miss Miller had that "disapproving look" on her face. I didn't skip a beat and finished to roaring applause from the girls, the other teachers. I knew I had this thing cinched and I think Mrs. Fredrigill thought so too. The meet was in two weeks and I couldn't wait to go.

Everybody went back to the classrooms and when it was time to go home Miss Miller called me into her living room. She had a stern look on her face. She said, "If you insist on giving that declamation at the meet, I'm not going to go with you."

I was stunned. "But I worked so hard on it. I know I can place with it," I argued.

She said, "Fine, go ahead. I'm not going to watch it."

I was heartsick, but it was more important to me to have her along and to please her, than it was to win this meet. She never told me why she didn't want me to do it. Carol was doing a far wilder declamation than that one, but she stood firm.

When I told Mrs. Fredrigill, she actually cried. She felt that Miss Miller was questioning her values and wondered if she had viewed the declamation as obscene. She agreed that, if Ruby disapproved, we should bag it, and we did. I quickly learned another speech and took it and "Sixteen" to the meet. Again, I got nowhere with the mundane stuff.

I was especially disappointed because the winner of the humorous category, who would go on to State, was a young fat kid that did, yeah, you guessed it, "The Speech Judge's Nightmare". Carol saw it and said he was really good, but didn't do it as well as I did. He didn't get the change in characters' voices very well. Carol took a second in her class that year. Everybody was really proud of her.

Looking back, I think Miss Miller had this idea of me as a lady, and that declamation really flew in the face of her perception of what she wanted me to present to the world. She never would let me play villains either, even though I asked her several times. She didn't get it, that I could be a lady and still function in different characters. I didn't resent the whole thing. It just made me sad. When I graduated I was a full-fledged, lifetime, Thespian.

While we were at the meet, we had lunch in the University

lunch room. A familiar voice rang out from across the room and here came my friend John, from the symphony. He was a freshman. I don't remember what his major was, but he minored in music, and was happy to see me. He got my address so he could write to me and later wrote me some wonderful long letters about school, and playing the clarinet in a jazz band.

It just dawned on me writing this, I never received one letter from my grandmother in Black Foot the whole time I was at the school. I know she and Miss Miller were in touch with each other, but she never wrote, or called me. She may have sent money though. I never wanted for anything. Between her and Miss Miller, they kept me in whatever I needed.

When we got back to the school, life went on. I was invited to John's parents' house one weekend. They lived near the dam outside of Helena. John's father oversaw the dam, and the people that worked there.

John came out and got me with his sister, the one who played the oboe. When we got to their house, they invited me inside and I was astonished. There was no carpeting on the shiny wood floor in the large living room.

There was a piano sitting near the big windows looking out over the huge dam. And there was a myriad of instruments- horns, winds, an accordion in the corner, Merrill's oboe in another corner. I think there were even some violins and guitars around. It was music heaven.

Chairs and music stands were scattered everywhere. This family all played instruments and they played them together. I've never seen anything like that before or since.

They sat down and played for me - blues, jazz, popular music, and classical. It must have been incredible to grow up like that. I'll never forget that family. They were very kind to me and I really envied their life style.

John referred to his clarinet as a licorice stick. I always thought that was funny. He played it like a professional. They all played like professionals. Playing music is what drove their lives and kept them together as a family. They got along really well and, obviously, loved each other deeply. It was one of the very fun experiences of my life.

By the time I was a senior I had lost touch with these people. The original conductor of the Helena Symphony had quit and they hired a new one. He was okay, but he wasn't magical like the other one. I soon tired of the whole thing and so did Mr. Porter, so we both quit, along with Sarah. It just wasn't fun any more.

Chapter 29

Ruby went on vacation two weeks out of the year, usually in the summer. I didn't know it then, but her niece told me she would go to Tacoma, Washington, where her sister and brother-in-law lived. She'd spend time taking courses on law at the University of Washington, as I said before, visiting with her sister, and taking her niece and nephew places. Martha, her sister, and she were very close, and their ashes are interned together in a Tacoma cemetery, along with Martha's husband.

I met one of the brothers once. He had come to the school to visit. I don't remember which one he was, but he had to have been at least six foot five inches tall. The whole family was tall except for Maud, the younger sister.

The brother was well built, but huge. He didn't quite have the aristocratic way about him that Ruby had, but he was very dignified and very friendly. He looked to be in his seventies and healthy as a horse. I was very flattered that she saw fit to introduce me to him.

Anyhow, it was summer. I had been in the school maybe two and a half years and it was a Saturday afternoon. The laundry was done, the chores were done, and we were all over at the Administration building watching a movie.

A few days before, several girls had decided they were going to do a daring runaway, led by a native girl we called "Louie". Her actual name was Lois. She was the queen of runaways. She did it just to see how far she could get and how many times she could do it. Her record, so far, was seventeen. She never really got anywhere.

She just liked the challenge.

Louie was small, maybe five feet tall, a hundred pounds soaking wet. She was slender, darkly pretty, fun and funny. And she had an adventurous spirit that carried her away, often into trouble.

Louie and her followers tied several sheets together and let them down out of the second story window of her room. How they got the heavy metal screening off the window I don't know, but they did.

One at a time the girls climbed down the sheets and headed for the horse pasture. The last girl got halfway down and the sheets tore. She landed on a pad of cement below and lay there with a broken leg. It was at least sixty feet to the ground and no mean feat for these girls to pull off.

Once the girls were out of sight in the pasture, a couple of them, who were left behind because of the torn sheet, went to get a matron to help the broken girl on the ground behind the building. She was hustled off to the hospital and came back on crutches, leg in a cast. She was lucky that's the worst that happened. That was a long fall.

Four of the runaway girls were brought back that Saturday while we were at the movies. Louie was one of them. They were sent to the recreation room in Canady Hall, and told to stay there until Arlette could decide what to do with them.

The girls decided it would be fun to cause some mischief, so they broke all the light bulbs in the ceiling of the rec room and the bathroom. They used a scrub board and had a great time shattering glass all over the place.

Gutsa was the matron on duty. She called Arlette to come over and calm the girls down. These were girls ages thirteen to maybe fifteen. The biggest one was maybe five foot three, and weighed a hundred ten pounds. The smallest was Louie and she was the oldest and the ringleader.

Arlette came to the cottage flanked by two of the three maintenance men. Both of them were big burly guys. She had tried to get Van, the head of the maintenance crew, to come as well. They were going to teach these girls a lesson. Van told her he was be damned if he was going to be involved in beating up on little girls and she could get him fired if she wanted to, but he wasn't going to participate.

So Arlette and the other two headed for Canady. When they got there, the girls were brought upstairs. Louie said later that she thought they were going to get the starch paddle and was geared up for that. When she saw the two guys, she knew this was going to be different.

The two men beat the hell out of all four of those little girls, with their fists. They pummeled the girls and the girls tried to fight back. The men were too strong for them. Arlette stood by the front door and laughed her big bellowing guffaw, while the girls screamed and tried to defend themselves.

Louie managed to get herself out of the grip of Brian's beefy fist and took a run at Arlette. She hit her in a head butt with her full weight, like a football player. Louie was so angry she wasn't feeling any pain.

The hit was so unexpected that Arlette didn't have time to brace herself and the big woman wound up flat on her butt on the floor. Then the men grabbed the little girl and pummeled her with their fists even harder.

When they were finished, they took the girls downstairs and threw them in the small dungeon at the end of the recreation room. It was a tiny, dark, dirty room, that hadn't been cleaned in years. There were bugs, spiders, and a dead rat on the floor.

When we got home from the movies we could hear the screaming coming from downstairs. We were told to mind our own business. The frightened girls screamed and cried all night. I guess this was supposed to be a warning to the rest of us, but all it did was make everybody angry and resentful.

When the girls were let out of the dungeon the next day, they told us what had happened. They were black and blue all over, especially Louie. She had a huge shiner, which totally closed her eye for several days.

There was talk among the girls of taking Gutsa down and beating the hell out of her. Several of us, with a little more sense, talked them into waiting until Ruby got home. We were going to tell her what Arlette and the maintenance men had done. Everybody trusted that she would make sure these monsters lost their jobs. We all knew that this was not a situation Ruby would have ever condoned.

When she got back to the school, Ruby did nothing about the beatings. I really believe Arlette went to the Governor before Ruby came home and told him why she did what she did and probably, building what the girls did into something a lot more serious than what it was.

I think the Governor sided with her, and Ruby had no say so in the matter. I know she was angry and walked around the school with a grim look on her face for a long time.

For the rest of the time while I was there, she didn't leave the school again for any length of time. Neither of the men lost their jobs and as far as I could tell, they weren't even disciplined for the part they played in the situation.

Lois ran away several more times after that, but now it wasn't the challenge. She got belligerent and wanted out. They finally stopped bringing her back.

I think Ruby was told she had to start using the dungeon. Some other girls got into trouble after the beating incident. She came over to see what was going on and one of them called her a "white-haired bitch". She sent them all to the dungeon, where they screamed profanities at her. She sat on a bench in the recreation room with her head hanging down and listened to them rave.

They swore and screamed at her for over an hour. I kept going up and down the stairs, checking on her, watching her emotionally bleeding to death over what she was doing. I don't think she even heard what they were screaming at her. I think she was just stunned at what she was doing.

She finally left the room and, incredibly, went to the kitchen and made a bunch of sandwiches. Then she went back downstairs, opened the dungeon door, and fed the same girls that had been cursing the ground she walked on. After giving them the sandwiches, she left and went back to the main building.

The next morning I went over to clean the breakfast dishes. Ruby sat in her winged-back chair in the living room and she was crying. She looked like hell. Her face was swollen and her eyes were red. Her big nose was red from blowing it. She looked up at me when I came in. She had the saddest look on her face and seemed stunned to see me standing there. She hadn't heard me come in. She quickly got up from her chair and went back into the bedroom.

I was heartsick for her. I have never before, or since, felt so sad for anyone as I did her. She had been forced to do, probably in her mind, the worst thing she had ever had to do to anyone. This was a lover of children and a protector of emotionally damaged children. Never in her life did she ever think she'd have to treat children with such cruelty. I'm really surprised she didn't quit her job right then and there.

I think the reality finally hit her of what kind of place the school was destined to become. She was such a gentle soul she couldn't bear the fact that she had had to use the dungeon with those girls. I don't think she'd ever in her life been treated like they treated her either.

There was one more incident where Ruby had to use the dungeon. I don't think I ever knew what those girls had done, but she wound up spraying them with the hose to get them to calm down. Then she closed the door again, leaving them soaking wet in that cold dreary dungeon. The place was rapidly losing its appeal for me.

Ruby was used to being admired and revered by children; not cussed out and threatened by them. In some respects, I do think she truly felt she was running a finishing school for girls, or at least trying to, until the more rowdy girls started being sent there.

She knew what prisons were about. The reality of what the school was becoming must have been a really hard pill for her to swallow. I don't think she saw her school as a prison until things started to go awry.

I mentioned "Chubby" earlier. She did have a name, Sylvia. However, she was short and heavy and in that place, she immediately got a nickname. She never complained about it and the nickname was never meant as a slur. It was just the automatic reaction the girls had with anyone unusual. Like me and the "Kid McCall" moniker.

Soon after coming into the school, one of the maintenance men took to calling me "Kid McCall" and that stuck. I was called "Kid" a lot by the girls.

Anyhow, Sylvia was one of the closest friends I ever made then or even now. She was very short, cute, blonde, blue-eyed, and heavy. She wore glasses, laughed easily, and followed me around like a puppy. We palled around together for a year and a half, shared the room in behind the matron's station, and even worked in the apartments together.

Our room was very large compared to the other girls' rooms. I don't know how we rated such a nice one, but we got it. I think it was one of the matrons' quarters. It even had a door.

I don't know how Sylvia wound up in a place like that. She wasn't even from Montana. She was from Washington State. I think she was visiting her dad, or living with him, or something. We never really talked much about her past.

She wasn't there long and got out before I did. I promised to come and see her when I got out, and I did. It sure wasn't the same. She was living with her mother and a couple of siblings and the whole visit was really clumsy and uncomfortable.

I left wondering how we could have been such good friends and not be able to relate at all on the outside. I guess it was such a closed environment in the school, even taste in people was different than on the "outside". Also, I think people want to forget they were in a reform school, and I was a reminder.

I ran into a couple of other people on the outside that were in the school with me and they wanted nothing to do with me either. Not even a "hi, how are ya". Too ashamed, I guess. I never was ashamed of being there. If I hadn't been sent there I probably would have wound up in prison, or killed on the streets somewhere. I've always been grateful that Mr. Jones cared enough to force the issue and have me placed out there.

Chapter 30

When I was seventeen, I was elected president of Canady Hall. I was a combination Junior/Senior, and would graduate that spring. I don't think the girls were pandering to me because of my relationship with Ruby. I think they looked up to me because I'd been there the longest and was one of the oldest girls there.

Being the president of the cottage didn't have a lot of meaning. It meant I took the blame when things went wrong. Also, I got to be a little bossy with the girls. It was a nice compliment for a loner like me, but it didn't hold much authority in a reform school.

The one and only fight I ever got into out there happened during that period. Some of us actors were in the Gym with Ruby and Mrs. Giulio, practicing "Huckleberry Finn". I had done my bit as "Puddinhead Wilson", another sweet good guy role and had gone to the back of the gym to sit with Alisha and Sarah. They were still into their lesbian period.

There were mattresses rolled up in the back of the gym used for gymnastics and we were sitting on them. I don't know what got into those two, but they decided that they wanted me to get sexual with them. That never happened before, or since. I didn't take kindly to their attempts to fondle me. I got really angry, hit one of them, and blindly left the gym, not telling anyone I was going.

I went back to Canady Hall, angry, humiliated, and looking for a fight. I couldn't believe Sarah, especially, would treat me that way, and it killed our relationship.

When I got back to the cottage I pounded on the big doors until a matron let me in. I stalked up the stairs headed for my room. As I walked down the hall to my room, I passed one of the rooms where a little girl, fairly new in the school, was sitting on her bed crying.

She'd been there maybe three months and was very young, maybe twelve or thirteen. She had a full set of false teeth already. She was pretty and small, and scared to death of her situation. She was another little native girl.

I walked into the room and sat down next to her. I put my arm around her and asked her why she was crying. She told me that Beulah Bear Head, the cottage bully at that time, had hit her in the mouth and broken her upper plate.

That was just the trigger I needed. Back came all the old anger and street-kid attitude, and I was ready to kill that bitch. I got up and stomped down the stairs, so angry my whole body felt hot. Never before, or since, have I ever wanted to kill someone, but I wanted to kill Beulah Bear Head.

I reached the living room and stood angrily in the doorway. I looked at Beulah and could feel my eyes burning a hole into her tiny brain. I shouted, "Beulah, get your ass out here. I want to talk to you."

"What?" she said innocently. "What did I do?"

Now, Beulah was not a small girl. She was probably fifteen or sixteen, short, maybe five feet two, and stocky. She probably outweighed me by thirty pounds. Everybody was afraid of her. She was aggressive and didn't care who she hurt. She was Native American and had a really nasty attitude. I'm not sure what she was in the school for, but it was probably something truly mean and nasty.

Beulah got up and came out into the entry hall. The hall was maybe twenty feet by twenty feet. At one end was the front door. At the other end were stairs going up to the bedrooms and down to the basement.

I stood glaring at the bully, then I screamed at her, "What in the hell did you think you were doing hitting little Sharon in the face? Do you realize you broke her teeth? What the hell is the matter with you?"

Beulah grinned stupidly at me and then she said, "I was just kidding around. It was an accident."

"Well," I said, still fuming. "You need to apologize to her. She's upstairs crying her eyes out."

Beulah was not the sympathetic type and wasn't about to feel remorse for anything she did. She gave me a look of disdain, chuckled, and turned to walk back into the living room. The girls, who had come out to watch the fray, parted to let her by. That was the wrong thing for her to do.

I grabbed her by the arm and spun her around, my anger turning to rage. "Don't you dare walk away from me when I'm talking to you, you bitch," I said much too quietly, venom dripping from my voice.

Girls were coming from all over the cottage now to watch this spectacle. Beulah turned back surprised, saw the look in my eyes, and knew she was in trouble.

She grabbed my arms and the fight was on. We wrestled each other to the carpeted floor and rolled around like a couple of frolicking puppies. Neither one of us tried to hit the other, which was strange for her. I had decided I would make her hit me first then I'd pummel her to death.

What I had in mind was, I was going to wrestle the big girl over to the stairs and roll her down them, hopefully breaking something, or killing her. By now, I wasn't concerned about getting hurt. I just wanted to hurt this girl, no matter what the cost. I wasn't thinking about the probability that I would go with her and could really get hurt, bumping down a flight of stairs with this big heavy beast on top of me.

This wasn't the good little lady that Ruby was trying to train me to be. This was the street kid that had kept me surviving for so many years, Kid McCall. She was enraged, and hurt and wanted to live again and run the show. I don't think Ruby really ever realized that that part of me existed and was always just below the surface.

I managed to work Beulah over to the stairs. We grunted and struggled, saying nothing. I'm sure the other girls were screaming and encouraging their favorite, but I didn't hear any of it. I was intent on murder.

The plan was to get her to the stairs and just hang onto her, throw myself over the edge, and start rolling. She was heavier than I thought and I had trouble moving her. Just about the time I had her on the stairs and was extricating myself from her grip, and getting ready to give her a mighty shove, the matron came running and she and some of the other girls pulled us apart.

Although I had the upper hand, Beulah shouted at me that I was lucky the matron stopped the fight, or she'd have beaten the hell out of me.

I yelled back at her, "Hey, let's go to the basement, bitch, and we can finish it there." She agreed, but the matron put the kibosh on the whole thing and sent us both to separate rooms to cool off. I sat down in the matron's sitting room and that's when I noticed I'd cut my shin badly on the metal guards that were on the edges of each step. The matron came and treated the cut. I still have a pretty good scar from that fight.

The next day, when I went over to do the breakfast dishes at the apartment, Ruby called me into her living room. She looked at me, checked out my leg, and said gently, "You need to leave the fighting with bullies to the bigger, tougher girls in the cottage." She smiled at me, patted me on the back, and sent me off to help finish the dishes. I think I saw some pride in her face.

I don't know if I could have beaten Beulah if we'd continued the fight. Once the rage died down, I probably wasn't all that strong and didn't like hurting people. I don't think she got hurt in the fight. To make excuses for her, some of her followers tried to claim she was pregnant and the fight caused her to have a miscarriage. That was crap and we all knew it.

However, Beulah never came near me again, was very respectful, and quit hitting little girls in the face. A couple of months later, she really paid the price for her bullying ways. Ruby got the little girl's teeth fixed and all was quiet for a while.

A new girl came into the cottage by the name of Stacey Cat Eyes. She was about fifteen years old and another Native American. She was slender, maybe five feet, four inches tall, and dark like the other native girls. Her hair was cut short and she had a soft, but strange, look in her dark eyes. I'm sure she was mentally ill and shouldn't have been placed there.

The reason she was there is that she had killed a man. She and a girlfriend were hitchhiking and some poor innocent guy picked them up. They were in the back seat of his car and her girlfriend dared her to kill him. Stacey carried a switchblade knife with her all the time. She simply took it out, reached around the guy's neck, and slit his throat with the knife. She didn't blink an eye, even when she told the story to us. She had no remorse, she didn't think it was a particularly odd thing to do, or even that it was funny. She just didn't seem to have any feeling about it at all. It was just a matter-of-fact thing she'd done to take a dare. It was frightening and eerie to think anyone would do a thing like that, especially a young teen-age girl.

I guess the Vocational School was the only place available to put a girl that young, so we wound up with her in Canady Hall. She wasn't a hard girl to get along with. She was quiet, somewhat of a loner, and she didn't talk too much to anyone most of the time. She just seemed to stay inside her own head and kept to herself.

The word around the cottage was, you don't wrestle around with Stacey in play. If you did, she couldn't hold onto her temper and she would seriously try to hurt you. Most everybody feared and respected her and left her alone.

I was visiting another girl in my old room one night. Stacey's room was two doors down the hall from that room. Beulah roomed with another girl in Eileen's and my old room next door.

I had my pajamas on and was getting ready to go back to my

room behind the matron's chair, when suddenly there was a comment floating in the air, coming from Beulah's room. A specter raced past the doorway and then there was a blood-curdling scream coming from next door. Girls came running from everywhere, including me.

When we got into the room, everybody's blood froze. Stacey had Beulah on the bed, and was sitting on her, smashing her in the face, over and over. When six of us managed to pull the raging girl off Beulah, her face was covered with small bloody holes. Stacey had been hitting her in the face with a pair of tweezers.

She was taken back to her room, and some girls sat with her until she calmed down. The matron on duty came running to see what was happening. By the time she got there, it was all over, but she took Beulah downstairs to treat the bloody holes on her face.

Beulah had made the mistake of making a comment about Stacey's mental health loud enough for Stacey to hear, and she went nuts. I'll guarantee you that that was the last time Beulah ever bullied anyone, or created any incidents again the whole time she was in the school. She was very lucky Stacey didn't kill her. I think she would have if she hadn't been pulled off the big girl. Beulah was no match for Stacey in a rage, even though she was half again as big as Stacey was.

Beulah was a bully, but she wasn't dangerous, barring an accident. Stacey was a killer and she was dangerous.

After I left the school, I came back to visit and spent some time with my old friend from way back when I was a little girl. Glenda had been sent out there about three or four months before I left. Why, I don't know. I never asked.

She was put into Canady Hall and she and I spent hours talking about how we were going to find her mother, get her off the streets, and sober her up. We had more schemes than a politician has trying to get elected. We would kidnap her and lock her up in our apartment, not letting her out until she'd been several months sober. We'd spirit her off to some halfway house and on and on it went.

I felt a little paranoid about having Glenda in the school. I was afraid Ruby would like her more than she liked me. I even asked Ruby if she would like a girl who played the piano better than I did, better than me. She smiled, looked puzzled then she assured me that it wouldn't make any difference to her how well someone played the piano.

When I went back after graduating, to visit, Glenda told me a hair-raising story. She had been cleaning the stairs one day and Gutsa got it into her head that Glenda hadn't done a good enough job. She made her do it over and over, three times and still, she wasn't satisfied.

Finally, Glenda sat down on the stairs, and refused to budge. Gutsa still didn't get it with these girls. Manhandling didn't work. It just made them madder and more belligerent. She grabbed Glenda's arm and tried to drag her off the stairs. In the process, she managed to cause Glenda to fall down about eight steps. She wasn't hurt badly, but she was stunned.

Stacey was coming out of the dining room and saw what was going on. She flew into a rage, ran back into the kitchen and grabbed a butcher knife. Before anyone could stop her she had Gutsa by the throat up against the wall with the knife against her jugular vein. Gutsa was screaming until Stacey's hand tightened around her throat and she couldn't breathe. Then she shut up and just stood there, eyes bulging out of her head.

She probably thought that this is how her reign in that school was going to end, and rightfully so.

Glenda ran back up the stairs to the basement that Gutsa had thrown her down and tried to talk Stacey off her. The girl was so entranced into what she was doing, Glenda told me, that she didn't think Stacey even heard her.

She stood there talking to the terrifying girl half afraid she might turn the knife on her, while another matron called Miss Miller. She raced over and somehow talked Stacey into giving her the knife. Stacey let a shaking Gutsa go and Miss Miller took the girl over to the main building. From there she was taken to Warm Springs, which was the state mental hospital.

Glenda and I never got to save her mother. A couple of years later, she went with some other folks to Fort Benton, all of them drinking heavily. She demanded they let her out of the car halfway between Great Falls and Fort Benton. They let her out and she went staggering down the highway trying to get back home. A state patrolman came speeding up over a hill, didn't see her, and hit her so hard he knocked her a hundred feet into a ditch. The medical examiner said it broke nearly every bone in her body.

The patrolman was never charged. He was doing ninety miles an hour, but there was no speed limit in Montana at the time. He never even sent condolences to the family.

Glenda's mom had been a beautiful woman in her youth. She played the piano, and that's probably where I developed the love for the instrument. By the time Glenda was in Junior High School her mom was on the streets and playing the piano in the taverns for drinks.

Glenda's dad was also a heavy drinker, but he continued to be able to take care of his daughter. As I said before, he and Glenda would take her mother home with them and try to sober her up. She'd last for about a week or two, then Glenda would come home from school and mom would be gone again. It was heartbreaking for all of them to lose her that way.

Chapter 31

As I said, I was a Junior/Senior. It was 1958, and there were four of us in the graduating class. There was a flurry of graduation pictures, fittings for graduation robes, new outfits to be bought, and, of course, sneak day.

Besides me there were Sarah, Jane (the little redhead that got us into a French class) and Barbara (a very shy quiet girl, very smart, who had the two sisters in the school with her). God only knows why they were there. All three were quiet, easy to get along with, and couldn't have done anything illegal. They just weren't the type. Her little sister was the eleven-year-old that tried to apologize to me for the nastiness of Cindy and Penny.

Barbara was probably the prettiest one of all four of us and maybe the smartest. It was hard to tell, she was so quiet.

Jane and I befriended each other during the last year I was in the school. She had a pretty singing voice and I liked to play the piano for her when she sang. We put together a rendition of the old song, "Ruby" and asked Miss Miller to come up to the auditorium, and we performed it for her.

There's a line in it that says, "Ruby, they say you're like a song. You don't know right from wrong". When we finished the song, she grinned at us and said, "I don't know about that. I think I know right from wrong". Then she turned and left the big room.

We were stunned. But, that's who she was. She'd enjoyed the music, but I think she was a little embarrassed and didn't know what to do with the feelings, so she joked her way out of it.

The matron got the four of us up at four o'clock in the morning. We got dressed and met Ruby in front of the administration building. We climbed into the blue station wagon and off we went in the dark for our Sneak Day. We had breakfast at an all-night diner and headed for Glacier Park. I later found out from her niece that Glacier Park was Ruby's favorite place in Montana. She loved to go there and wander around in the beauty and wonder of the place.

Her niece, telling me that, made the trip just that much more special. I don't remember much about it. I just loved being with her and it didn't matter much where we went. I do remember the "Going to the Sun" highway. It wound up a steep mountainside with switchbacks and drop offs. It was beautiful and very scary.

We five spent the day driving through the park, stopping to look at bears and elk, and to admire the scenery. We had lunch and headed back to Helena late that afternoon.

A few days later Mrs. Fredrigill, the English teacher, had us draw straws for who would be Valedictorian. Sarah drew the longest straw, so she gave the speech. Barbara, Jane, and I spent hours helping Sarah practice.

Miss Miller wanted some of my relatives to attend the graduation. I told her it wasn't a big deal to me, but she persisted. Did she want to show them I was worthy of them? I don't know. She tried to get my mother's brother Bob and his wife to come out and watch me graduate. They lived in Helena. They told her they had a picnic to go to that day and couldn't attend.

The truth was, Bob's wife couldn't tolerate the idea that she had a relative that was in a reform school. She worked for the Capitol so she knew Miss Miller. She was really into appearances and she wasn't going to subject herself or her kids to "bad girls".

Miss Miller sounded very disgusted with them when she told me they wouldn't be coming. I told her I didn't care. All that mattered to me was that she would be there looking proud. She still didn't seem to get it, that she had become my family and all I really wanted was for her to be there.

I look back on that situation and, knowing what I do today about how important family was to her, I can see why it was so important to her that some of my relatives be there. She didn't understand not having close, caring family members. It just didn't compute for her.

The graduation went well. They graduated the eighth graders first. Then the band played music and I played something on the piano. I ran back, while the chorus sang, and put on my robe. Mrs. Giulio started the graduation march.

I had played the march for the graduation the year before and now she was playing it for me and two of my friends. We all four felt very proud walking down the middle of all those town people seated in the gym. We were the big deals that day.

Miss Miller stood on the stage and watched us walk to the first rows of chairs and sit down. She gave an introduction, and Sarah got up and gave her speech. When Sarah sat down, Miss Miller handed out the diplomas with a proud smile for each of us. Then it was over.

The other three girls went over to the cottage to get their

things and head home with their families. I wasn't sure what to do. The plan was that I was to go to Dillon in the fall and attend the normal school there. Miss Miller wanted me to go there. She wanted me to become a teacher. I guess I thought I would stay at the school until I left for Dillon. This was not to be.

My mentor called me into her living room and told me I needed to get packed and ready to go into Helena. She was going to take me to a motel in town to work until it was time to go to Dillon. I was stunned. I started to cry and begged her to let me stay at the school. She got upset and became stern-faced and anxious. She said, "I can't let you stay here once you graduate. You have to leave." Again, I wasn't prepared for what was going to happen to me. I was just told. I could feel myself shutting down emotionally. The tears stopped and I left to get packed.

She took me to Helena the next day. The lady that ran the motel was young, had a husband, and maybe a child or two. I don't remember much about her. She was nice.

I was given a room. Miss Miller gave me her little 45 record player and all the records that went with it. I settled in and she left.

Before she went, she told me she would come in the next day and take me to the music store where I'd be taking organ lessons. Why she set that up, I have no idea. Something to keep me busy, I guess. So, the next day, I started organ lessons.

When I wasn't working in the motel, cleaning rooms, I was listening to records, going roller skating, and being lonely. I met a kid, Jack, at the roller rink and we began dating. He had been real popular in school. His grandmother worked for the governor's office. I think she might have been his secretary. She hated that Jack was dating me.

He was a fun kid and a good dancer. He had won a Rock and Roll contest with a little rich girl from Helena. We went skating and hung out at the old Parrot Café. It was all pretty innocent. His grandmother was having fits.

One night Miss Miller came to the motel and told me to stop seeing him. This was the only time she ever came to visit me. When I wanted to know why she wanted me to stop seeing him, she told me the grandmother had called her and told her she didn't want Jack hanging out with "one of those girls".

Miss Miller told her that Jack wasn't good enough for me. The grandmother told her that "she just didn't understand because she'd never had any children of her own".

Miss Miller responded, "You're right, I don't have any children of my own. I've been too busy raising everybody else's kids."

For the first time, I stood up to this woman I thought of as mom. I wasn't being belligerent. I was being my own person again. I felt alone and abandoned again and she wasn't going to tell me what to do. I told her no, I wouldn't stop seeing Jack until I decided I didn't want to see him any more, and that old bitch of a grandmother could go to hell. She looked a little surprised at my stand, but she accepted it and left. I don't remember her ever coming back to visit me.

I hung out with Jack all summer. It was the first time I'd had a real boyfriend. He was my first real sexual experience and I was his. There was nothing exciting to report there. Neither one of us could figure out what the hell the fuss was all about.

I had made up my mind I didn't want to be institutionalized

again, and that's what I thought college would be all about. I only had the one friend, Jack, in Helena, and I wouldn't have anyone in Dillon. I knew nothing about school outside the Vocational School, so I assumed college would be the same. Miss Miller had no idea how my mind was working and she didn't think to ask.

When I told her I didn't want to leave Helena that year, she didn't argue. She just packed me up and moved me to the YWCA. She, or Arlette found me a job working as a policy typist for Western Life Insurance Company, which was across the street from the YWCA. Again, she settled me and left. I think she was angry and disappointed, but, at that point, I don't think I cared much. She was just someone else moving in and out of my life and not leaving any tracks.

Meanwhile, Jack had decided we should get married. I was still only seventeen, and pretty naïve. I really didn't want to marry the kid, but he'd bought me an engagement ring with the money he was saving up to buy a car. I accepted it reluctantly. His mother decided she'd better get acquainted with me. His grandmother had apoplexy.

Jack was excited and I was dead inside. I really didn't want this situation, but I had no one to talk to that could help me figure out how to get out of it. So, I finally talked Jack into going into the Army. I don't remember much about that conversation. He hadn't finished high school and I think I convinced him that the Army would help him learn a skill so he could support me, or something.

Anyhow, his mom, grandmother, and I saw him off on the train and I went back to the YWCA, and work. A couple of weeks later, I wrote him a "Dear John" letter, and sent his ring back. Unfortunately, I sent it in an envelope and all he got was the letter and the envelope with a hole in it. That might have been a mean thing to do, but he didn't realize how lucky he was. I proceeded to go nuts and he didn't have to deal with it.

I was at the roller rink one night and I thought I saw Dave, the Youth for Christ minister skating around. I skated up behind the guy, slapped him on the back, and said, "Let's see you do your fancy stuff."

Well, it wasn't Dave and he wasn't a very good skater. The blow to the back sent him stumbling and sliding and he landed hard on his rear end. I helped him up, apologizing all over the place. We skated and talked the rest of the night.

The guy's name was Bob. He told me he worked in construction on a building down town near the Western Life building. He said he had seen me walk by several times and had always wanted to talk to me. He was a nice guy, drove a 1950 Mercury, (very cool car), laughed easily and he drank. I got to hanging out with him, and drinking. The booze eased the loneliness and the pain of losing Ruby. Bob was devoted and good company.

Then, the job at Western Life went east. They moved the whole company to Minnesota, or somewhere. All who worked for them were invited to go along and, I suppose some did. I wasn't leaving Helena, so I moved in with Bob.

We moved into an apartment on the second floor of a huge old house. Bob worked and we drank. He bought a 1953 customized Ford with black and white leather interior. It had a 1956 Oldsmobile three-quarter-race engine in it and a 1946 Buick stick on the floor. That car was the second hottest car in Helena. It was a beautiful lavender color with whitewall tires and all the chrome removed.

People stared when it rumbled by. And it rumbled like a beast getting ready to attack. I felt like the coolest person in Helena when I drove that car.

The only downside to the car was the reverse in the transmission was gone. I loved to take the car and pull into the town drive-in where all the kids hung out. They'd walk around the thing and just gaze at it. I felt so cool. However, when I decided to leave, they had to all get together and push me out of the parking space. Then I'd throw her into gear, and tear out of the parking lot, speed-shifting as I went, throwing gravel everywhere.

The only thing I didn't do was the evil laughter as I flew out into the night, screaming through the gears. Eat your hearts out, kids!

I loved to take the car out into the Helena Valley. The road ran straight as an arrow for miles. I could open the car up a far as I dared, and just fly.

One night Bob, myself, and another couple took the car out to the Valley Highway. Bob wanted to see how fast the thing would actually go. Of course we'd been drinking. He opened the lavender beast up and, at 110, it started to float. The body was just too lightweight to support that powerful an engine. The car wanted to take off like a plane.   Bob didn't like the feel of it, so, even though I was into the thrill and wanted to go even faster, he started slowing the car down. His two friends in the back looked like their faces had been doused in plaster. As Bob slowed it down, the car started to bump along the highway, and soon he could hardly keep it on the road.

He pulled over and stopped. The guys got out and found two flat tires. It's a miracle we all weren't killed. I don't know how he kept it on the road long enough to stop it. Like any teen, I didn't see the danger. It was just an exciting thing to have happen. I was totally oblivious to the death card not being dealt that night.

I was a real mess, anyway.   I would drive the Ford around town with a quart of beer between my legs and a cigarette hanging out of my mouth. I'd gone back to smoking, maybe trying to get even with Ruby. Bob and I were doing a lot of drinking.

I'd be driving down Last Chance Gulch, the main street in Helena, cruising with the other kids. Suddenly, I'd let go of the wheel, yell "chicken" and hit the gas. The first one to grab the wheel was chicken. Bob always was first to grab the wheel. I didn't care.

I'd had my license for a very few short months. I'd known how to drive for years, but, after practicing with a 1953 Chevy Coupe that Bob borrowed from a friend, I took my driving test in it. I couldn't get a smooth shift from first to second gear in that car, so I shifted from first to third and the tester said nothing about it. He passed me.

It's a wonder I didn't lose my license and wind up in jail the way I was functioning. How I survived this period, I don't know. I know I was suicidal, but I wasn't aware of it at the time. I just went with the flow.

Bob was a good caring guy when he was sober, and scary and mean when he was drunk. One night, he was very drunk, and wound up sitting on me with his fist balled up, threatening to hit me. A friend of his was there and stopped him. I ran outside and locked myself in the car. He came out and ran around the car, leering at me and beating on the windows. It scared me to death. He stopped drinking after that, probably afraid he would beat me up and really hurt me.

He took me to a dance a couple of weeks later and, to show how tough I was, I chug-a-lugged a pint of whiskey. I found myself in the bathtub throwing my guts up all night, with Bob and his friend trying to clean me up and keep my bandaged arm dry. They debated taking me to the hospital, but were concerned about what would happen to them, because I was underage. I survived and the drinking slowed down.

My whole left arm was bandaged because of a silly accident, a couple of nights before the drinking incident. I had been playfully chasing Bob through the apartment. He ran into the bedroom and slammed the French doors. I went to push them open and accidentally hit the glass. I sliced my arm open and just stood staring at the blood gushing, in shock. Bob put a tourniquet on it and raced me to the emergency room. It took several stitches to close the wound.

Bob came home one day with an old 1946 Buick coupe. He was going to take the transmission out of it and put it into the Ford. The only problem with the old car was that the brakes didn't work on it. You had to gear it down and then, literally, drag your foot to stop it.

Hey, that didn't stop me from driving the thing. I drove it all over Helena and thought the braking system was funny. Helena is situated on a very hilly area. One day, a girlfriend and I decided to take the old car and drive it down the main street of town. This meant getting down a steep hill.

The street ended on Last Chance Gulch, the main street running through town. There were stores lining the street. I eased the car in low gear down the hill, but when we reached the bottom, we couldn't get the thing stopped. The old coupe slowly rolled across the street and onto the sidewalk. We barely missed landing in the window of a liquor store before we managed to get it stopped. We backed back onto the main street and continued our drive down the busy road.   Hey, the reverse worked!

We were stopped again by a cop. This time we managed to stop without dragging feet. Sometimes, if you pumped the brakes real hard, the car would stop. We sat waiting, while another police officer tried to guide the governor's wife into a parallel parking space. The traffic on both sides piled up as we waited and waited and, after the third try, she finally succeeded and we went on our way. Yes, the same wife, the one with the mink stole.

Bob decided we should get married. I figured, why not? I didn't understand marriage, nor did I have much respect for it. My mother had been married at least eight times by then and the whole exercise was meaningless to me. But, if he thought we should, then what the hell? I didn't have anything better to do.

So, he and I and his two friends, headed out for Great Falls one day to tie the knot. We went to the courthouse there and were married by a Justice of the Peace. I was so oblivious to what was going on, that I didn't even realize I wasn't marrying a Cantrell. I was marrying a Rowin. Bob had changed his name after he got out of prison and never said anything to me about it.

I didn't find out about my married name until many years later when I tried to get a copy of my social security card. I was stunned.

When a living thing is programmed into a certain way of being, it's there for life. Even though that programming can be altered by education, a different training program, and different circumstances, when left without guidance, it will go back to the initial programming for survival. That's exactly what I did.

I got involved with a guy who couldn't settle down and was constantly on the move, reminiscent of my life with my mother. We lived in an upstairs apartment in a huge house in Helena. We drank and played with cars. We played like kids, teen-agers. Of course, I was a teen. I was still only 17.

I understand why Ruby gave up on me, but, it's still sad to think about. I was still having trouble with my mother. She lived in Helena and every time I got a job, she'd come in and hang around. I was washing dishes in a restaurant and she'd come in and just sit at the counter. They finally asked me to leave to get rid of her.

I tried to apply for a job as a secretary with a loan company. My mother happened to be walking by, saw me inside interviewing, and stood waving at me from outside. The manager asked me who that was. When I told him, he, in a nice way, said that he couldn't hire me because his business couldn't handle my mother hanging around. It was very embarrassing. I wasn't going to do well in Helena with her there.

Anyhow, Bob decided we needed to go to Oregon and I was

totally willing. We packed up the old 1941 Chevy coup and off we went. I don't know what happened to the Ford or the Buick. Didn't ask, didn't care. It was getting toward winter and snow was falling in the passes. I drove that old car, no snow tires, across the pass between Idaho and Montana in the middle of the night in a blizzard with Bob sleeping in the back. Back then it was a two-lane highway with no guard rails. I'd be scared to death to do that today, even with my four wheel drive!

We stayed with friends of Bob's in Portland for a while. We got jobs working at a boarding kennel where I first learned about electric fences. We had taken Trixie, my mother's old dog with us because she had no place to keep her.

One day I was moving some dirt in a wheelbarrow and had Trixie sitting on top of the dirt. I pushed the wheelbarrow under an electric wire, got it stuck, and pulled back to get some leverage. Trixie's neck was pushed against the wire and I was, unceremoniously, knocked on my butt. Bob saw the whole thing and literally fell on the ground laughing. I couldn't see the humor in it at the time. I definitely do now. Oh, by the way, it didn't have any effect on the dog.

We went from Portland to Corvallis, and Bob found a job driving shaving trucks. The trick was to get loads from the sawmill to the fiber board company as fast as possible. You were paid by the load.

This job was right up my alley. I soon got my own truck and I would actually race the other guys with my load and usually bring in at least one more load a day than they did. The trucks had tall boxes on them making them top-heavy. You'd see a shaving truck racing around a corner tipping on two wheels and the driver would just keep on hitting that gas. I was guilty of doing that sometimes myself. I never saw a paycheck and never asked about it. Bob took care of all of that.

I even tried to chew Copenhagen once when I was driving. It wasn't bad, but spitting out the window, like Bob could do, didn't work out well for me. I had long flowing hair and after landing a pretty good chaw in my hair, I decided to stick to smoking cigarettes.

During that period, Bob took me to Salem, Oregon to see his mother, who was in the state mental institution there. She was a big woman, maybe five feet nine or ten inches tall, short, nearly black hair with a bad haircut. Bob didn't resemble her much, except for the dark hair and the thick eyebrows. He was short and slender.

His mom mostly stared into space and talked about her son Peter, which I thought was strange. Bob kept telling her he was her son, but she didn't seem to recognize him.

The attendant told us the doctors had done a lobotomy on the woman and she just wasn't home any more. They said she just got too hard to handle and was strong as an ox, so they destroyed the emotional part of her brain.

She had been there since Bob was about seven or eight years old. His father, who was short, squat, and very powerful, had been killed in a timber accident. His father was her life line. He had taken her out of a very abusive situation with her father when she was seventeen, had nearly beaten her father to death to get her away, and he was her white knight.

When Bob's father was killed, his mom tried to jump off the Newport, Oregon bridge and wound up in Salem. Her beautiful long black hair had been cut up around her ears and she was gone.

Bob walked away in tears, and I don't think I'd ever felt so sorry for anyone as I did him at that point. Of course, because I didn't relate to anyone very well, it didn't last long. I did wonder why she kept talking about Peter. I thought Bob was an only child.

Bob told me about his dad. He said the guy was a very protective and loving father. One day, Bob came home from school all beaten up from the older kids. He'd tried to fight back and really got beaten up even worse. He was smaller than the other kids and didn't have a chance.

The next day, out on the school yard during recess, the kids started up with Bob again. Suddenly, as he tried to back away from them, he found his dad behind him holding a baseball bat. His dad handed him the bat and said, "You need an equalizer". He handed Bob the bat, backed off and watched his little son, "thump some heads". Needless to say, the kids didn't bother him again after that.

We went to work in the peach canneries there in Corvallis for a while. At one time, I was working two jobs and Bob was driving truck.

Then, for some reason, we weren't working any more. The

peach season ended, I guess. I didn't ask, just went with the flow.

During that period, we lived in a little apartment, had no money, and no food. I have no idea why. I was so depressed I took an overdose of aspirin, thinking it would kill me. I had tried iodine once and it didn't work. Bob took me to the hospital and the next day a social worker came in and gave me hell. She didn't ask me why I took the pills, she just gave me hell.

The lady in the next bed was a very sweet, probably middle class, woman in her sixties. She told me that when she got depressed she would work all day to make her husband a wonderful dinner and that would make her feel better. I had two potatoes in my house and nothing else. Her advice left me cold.

Bob found another job working on a sheep ranch outside of Corvallis, Oregon. We lived in an old farmhouse there and I spent hours wandering with my dogs through the woods. I raised a black lamb whose mother abandoned it and it eventually became the lead ram in the flock. I had five dogs, a piano, which Bob had bought, and things were good. I was depressed, as usual, but not suicidal.

I wrote and told Ruby about my life. I told her about the young fawn my dogs had found. I took it home and had it for about a week, when the mother came out of the woods and claimed it. I've always been told that, once human scent is on a fawn, the mother won't take it, but this one came after the baby and they bounded off together.

I told her about the Great Dane I had adopted. She had been given to me because she wouldn't let the postman deliver the mail. She didn't growl at him. She just sat in front of the box, and wouldn't let him near it. He was intimidated and complained.

When I'd take her out, she'd pace deer. She wouldn't chase them, she'd pace them, tongue lolling out of her mouth, loping along beside them. Then she'd tire and come back. The deer didn't seem to fear her. I'm not sure they weren't enjoying wearing out that big oaf of a dog.

I'd never been allowed to have a pet, so I sure made up for it. I had five dogs. And I loved every one of them.

The owner of the farm also raised wheat. He let me plow and work one of his fields. I had a great time driving round and round that field, pulling a plow and a harrow. I'd daydream about rescuing Debbie Reynolds from her sadness at the loss of her husband, Eddie

Fisher to Elizabeth Taylor.

I also got to drive combine for a while, but the farmer got irritated because, being the speed demon I was, I'd drive it too fast and most of the grain was overshooting the truck, landing on the ground on the other side. So that job didn't last long.

Ruby wrote me back and said we reminded her of the couple in "The Egg and I". After reading the book, I'm not sure which couple she meant. I could have been either, except for the kids. We never even had a pregnancy.

That winter, it rained hard, and the whole damn place flooded. The barn and the house sat on high ground and were spared, but you couldn't get anywhere because of the deep water. And sheep are so stupid. The whole bunch of them crowded into a corner of the fence as the water rose up and up.

Bob and I took a rowboat that was on the place and literally pulled every one of those thirty or more sheep out of the water and rowed them to the high ground by the barn. We saved them all. None of them drowned.

I bought Ruby a Glenn Miller album after I got her letter. I was so happy to hear from her and wanted her to know how much I still loved her. I didn't hear back from her, but about a week later Arlette called me to tell me Ruby had died. She said Ruby got the album while she was in the hospital and was really happy to receive it. I asked her for Ruby's Science and Health book and Arlette sent it. I fell apart and wanted to die.

I couldn't go to her funeral. It was held at the school. I just couldn't bring myself to truly admit she was gone.

That summer, my mother showed up unannounced and wanted to stay with us. It worked out okay, until Bob told me she'd been hanging out in a restaurant in Junction City and had told several people that he was a peeping tom, for crying out loud. He was upset, but not nearly as upset as I was. She was going to ruin things again.

I confronted her the next morning and she went nuts. She literally attacked me with a pair of scissors. I managed to take them away from her, grabbed her purse, and led her to the door by her hair. She twisted and fought and screamed all the way, but I got her out the door.

Unfortunately, the door had a big window in it and she

smashed it with her purse, cutting her arm pretty good. She walked out to the old country road and sat there looking broken. I felt so sorry for her I went and got her, bandaged her arm and, when Bob got home, I drove her to the bus station and sent her back to Montana. I couldn't wait for that big Greyhound to turn the corner and drive out of sight with her in it.

Chapter 32

Shortly after that, Bob decided we should go to California, so we packed up the old Chevy, gave away all but two of the dogs and were on our way to Sacramento.

There he got a job milking cows. We stayed in a small apartment with an old prison buddy of his. Soon, that job was gone and he moved on to a car lot. He sold cars and I worked in a gas station pumping gas and washing windshields. Yes Virginia, there were such places back then.

We lived in a motel for a while during that period. One night, I went nuts. I wasn't even drinking, just bitter, angry, and crazy. We argued about something, who knows what and I chased

Bob out into the parking lot brandishing a very long deadly butcher knife. I had every intention of killing him. All my anger, fears, loneliness, and resentments came to the surface and he got the full brunt of it.

I slashed at him and abruptly came to my senses when I slit the shirt he was wearing, leaving a very red, but not bleeding line down his back. It scared him and me. I stopped myself, put the knife down and we went on with our lives. I can't imagine why he stayed with me after that. It had to be terrifying.

Maybe he thought I was his punishment for what he'd done to land in prison. He and Don had stolen some equipment, chain saws, and some other stuff. I don't remember what all. They had left it with a guy in Montana and when they went back to get it, they found he had sold it.

They took the man out on an old country road in the woods in the middle of winter, made him take his shoes off, put him out of the car, and, making him walk barefoot in the snow, shot real bullets at him. Bob told me Don wanted to kill the guy, but Bob wasn't willing to go to prison for murder and the guy was pleading with him to help him. So, back into the car they put him, and took him back to town. The guy turned them in to the police.

Don had been a Jeep thief when he lived in L.A. He was fourteen. He'd steal a Jeep, drive it around until it was nearly out of gas then push it off a cliff somewhere outside of L.A. He was never caught. He always thought that was pretty funny.

One day, I was hanging out with Bob in the car lot and his friend Don came driving in with a really neat dove-white 1955 or '56 Mercury, covered with shimmering chrome, whitewall tires and slick white leather interior. He sat there with a stupid grin on his face as Bob and I walked around the car admiring the style and the beauty.

The car sat, engine rumbling like a roll of distant thunder, waiting for its orders to tear out of that lot, tires screaming and smoking in protest. Don, looking very cool said, "Listen to this engine. It's the biggest, fastest one they make."

With that he hit the accelerator full down, the engine roared like an angry bull, screamed, and then clattered with a sound like someone had just dropped a garbage can full of tin cans from a three-story building.

Don's face went from confusion, to horror, to a blank stare. Bob was rolling on the ground laughing and holding his sides. I just laid across the hood of Don's beautiful, useless car and howled with laughter. The rods had gone clear through the pan. Oil was pouring out of every orifice of that engine. I've never seen such a sorrowful look on anyone's face. This was one of the few cars that Don didn't steal. They called for a tow, and he watched miserably as his dream car was towed away.

There was a little old black man that worked for the car lot washing cars. He'd been there for years. He had a wife that absolutely dwarfed him in weight and height.

She kept the keys to their car, kept a chain and padlock on the refrigerator, and made him walk seven miles to and from work every day except payday. She'd drive him in to collect his paycheck, leave, and she wouldn't be seen again until the next payday.

To me he seemed like he was living in slavery. One day we sat talking and he told me about the refrigerator. I asked him why he would stay with someone like that. His answer was, "She needs me and I need to be needed." Boy, could I relate to that.

Suddenly, out of nowhere, Bob decided he wanted to go back to Oregon. We had an old Nash Rambler, the kind that made down into a bed. Also, I had bought a 1950 maroon-colored Studebaker convertible. It could move like greased lightning. The only problem it had was it burned a quart of oil ever fifteen or twenty miles. Black smoke would just pour out of that thing, as it flew down the road.

I loved it. When we took off, Don and Bob drove the Nash and I flew along in the convertible, stopping at every town to buy used oil to fill the thing up. It was great on gas though.

Somewhere between Sacramento and Redding California a cop finally pulled me over. He asked me if I was trying to oil the highways. Then he wanted my driver's license. I didn't have one and told him so. My Montana license had expired and I never bothered to get another one.

The cop gave me a break. He had Don drive the convertible and I was to ride with Bob. When we crossed into Oregon I was back in the driver's seat of the Studebaker. The rods finally went out in Corvallis and Bob sold the car to a kid for fifteen dollars.

Don left and went back to California and Bob got a job

working in a peach orchard. There was a house on the property that we lived in.

During this time, I had reconnected with Ron, the guy from Havre. He was remarried, but he told me on the phone that if I came back he'd like to get together again.

I didn't realize it but I was desperate for some stability. Living in cars, on beaches, in motel rooms, and wherever was no different than the way I'd lived with my mother. I wanted a home, family. I wanted kids and normal stuff. I couldn't put it into words what my needs were. Maybe if I had Bob would have settled down. I wasn't in touch enough with myself, or normalcy, to understand.

I daydreamed about marrying Ron, having kids, and being a mom. It never dawned on me that I might have been able to have that with Bob. Ron represented stability to me. The school had been the only safety and security I'd ever known and I wanted it again. Ron was the only other person I'd had any experience with that seemed to have staying power.

I told Bob I wanted him to take me back to Montana. I wanted to go be with Ron. He didn't get angry, abusive, nothing. He just said he would take me when he could.

The peach orchard wasn't paying much, if anything. Bob would go to town in the little Nash and come home with a bag of groceries and the inevitable carton of cigarettes for me. He didn't smoke.

The way he'd pull this off with no money was he'd pick up a paper bag when he walked into a grocery store, and start filling it up. Then he'd just walk out. No one would say a word.

I learned to go into a store and tell them I'd bought a ham a couple of days prior, and it was rank. I couldn't bring the wrapper back because it stunk so badly. I'd tell the clerk I'd paid eight or nine dollars for the ham and they'd reimburse me. That was one of the ways we got money for gas. The other way was what Bob called the "Okie credit card". We'd hit the construction sites with a gas can and a siphon hose.

I wanted so badly to go back to Montana that I got vicious with Bob. I had a switchblade knife that I liked to practice throwing at targets. Two inches short of Bob's face became the target. He'd be working on or near a tree and, suddenly, the long blade would softly swish past his face and imbed itself in the thick bark. When he turned to look at me I'd just stare at him, pull my knife out of the tree, and walk away.

I told him to never sleep too soundly. You never knew what could happen when you were sleeping and living with someone who hated you. I know now his heart must have been shredding from this sudden change in attitude toward him. He wasn't particularly stable but he did love that crazy young girl.

One night, we were sleeping. I rolled over and Bob, so frightened by now of me, sat bolt upright in the bed and shook. He thought I was moving on him and was going to knife him. The next day we headed for Montana.

He dropped me and my deaf German Shepherd off in Havre. My mother was living in a little basement apartment there. Three days later the dog jumped the fence, and I never saw it again.

-To Be Continued-

Made in United States
Orlando, FL
21 April 2023